Conversations With A Masterpiece,

Miracles and Medical Marvels!

The valleys I have walked through...
The shadows of death I have conquered...
The miracles I have experienced!

A factual book of my incredible life!

by Steven W. Cooke

**100% of proceeds from this book go to
HealthQuest House Foundation**

Steven W. Cooke

8-'08

Table of Contents

Acknowledgments I

I would like to publicly acknowledge all of the medical professionals who have dedicated their lives to saving lives. Endless hours of study for the enhancement of human life have been committed, and will continue to be committed, by these wonderful medical professionals. The medical profession is undoubtedly one of the most worthy, other-centered careers anyone could desire.

I wholeheartedly appreciate and respect the following medical professionals and medical institutions. Their significant expertise to the organ transplant community and their willingness to go above and beyond what most humans can only imagine is highly respected! The following medical professionals who helped to save my life are listed in chronological order, followed by the organ transplant medical centers where my life was saved:

Dr. Andre Minuth
Dr. Oscar Salvatierra
Dr. Nicholus Fuduska

Dr. Flavio Vincinti
Dr. William C. E. Amend
Dr. William Gish
Dr. Stephen Steady
Dr. Adil 'Ed' Walkeil
Dr. Robert Osario
Dr. Christopher Freise
Dr. John Roberts
Dr. Jimmy Roberts
Dr. David Potter
Dr. Douglas Anderson
Dr. Stephen A. Vannucci
Gloria Horns, R. N., B.S.N., J.D.
Karen Devaney, R.N., M.S.N.

University of California San Francisco, Moffitt Medical Center, Kidney Transplant Surgeons, Physicians, Nurses and staff.

California Pacific Medical Center, Pacific Campus, Liver Transplant Surgeons, Physicians, Nurses and staff.

Chico Cancer Center, Infusion Therapy, Chico, California

DaVita South, Hemodialysis Center, Chico, California

Acknowledgements II

I would also like to publicly acknowledge my family and friends who are just as important as the previous acknowledged medical professionals for helping to save my life and for my continued success.

Stacey Cooke
David Cooke
Frank T. Cooke
Betty Cooke
Michael Cooke
Frank Cooke, Sr.
Hilda Cooke
Joyce (Cooke) Moser
Connie (Cooke) Kinnee
April Lynn
Bill Lynn
Ann Averil
Mary Averil
Jim McIlvain
Tracy Tice

Nancy Tice
John Jans
Gordie Varney
Lynn Varney
Luisa Garza
Linda Twehous
Terri Gardner
Cathy Olmo
Michael Decker
Dominic Nastri
Patricia Nastri
Pastor Steve Grandy
Pastor Michael Christian
Northern California Organ Transplant Support
    Group, Chico, California
Steven Horne and Joesph Miceli, Merit Medi-
    Trans, Chico, California
GOD!

I would like to thank Mr. Dominic Nastri for the outstanding job he did with the beautiful drawings throughout my book. Mr. Nastri lives in the tall pines of Paradise, California, and sells his work mostly in Northern California. Mr. Nastri does wonderful acrylic paintings of wildlife and portraits. If you would like to purchase original paintings or prints or to see more of Mr. Nastri's lovely work, please go to my website and click on PRODUCTS at:

www.healthquesthouse.com

or contact Mr. Nastri at 5922 Sawmill Road, Paradise, California 95969.

I also want to thank Assistant Pastor Michael Christian of Jubilee on the Ridge church in Paradise, California, for pre-editing my book and being a great incentive to finish it. This book would not have been possible if not for his dedication and time.

The last person I want to acknowledge is Sheryl Lawson. A tremendous thank you goes to Sheryl of Paradise, California for putting in a great amount of time conducting the interview.

Dedication

"This book is dedicated to all the wonderful families who said "YES" to organ donation and started their legacy of love! Even though their loved one has passed on to Heavenly places, their loved one is still cherished and deeply loved in their heart and also within an extremely grateful person who received the 'GIFT OF LIFE'. May God bless each donor family member and your loved one who has passed on before you.

I want to acknowledge and honor the loved ones who said "YES" to organ donation in 1976, and I received their loved one's kidney. I do not know the name of my kidney donor. I do not know anything about my wonderful donor other than approximately when they died and that they gave me another chance at life. I do love them for saving my life by saying "YES" to organ donation.

I also want to acknowledge and honor the Holguin family of Central California. In 1997 they said "YES". Their precious daughter, Anita Maria Holguin, was a passenger in a horrible auto accident. She now lives on towards greatness within me. I received her liver and many other grateful patients received other life saving organs from her. I love the Holguin family with all my heart.

Turning tragedy into triumph is 'OTHER-CENTERED LOVE'. It's an accident that happens… it's a tragedy when the accident happens to you or a loved one. The Bible tells us to love our neighbors as ourselves. Donating life is the ultimate of OTHER-CENTERED LOVE."

Steven W. Cooke

Introduction

～

"This is a factual account of the miracles and medical marvels that have happened in my life. I have solely written this book by myself without a ghost-writer or co-author. I'm here with my book not to change your view, but, to give you another angle to view from. I write this book as inspiration for those involved in the organ transplant world, especially for the organ transplant patient awaiting a life-saving organ transplant. This book is for every organ transplant patient, organ transplant recipient, organ transplant support personnel, organ transplant medical professionals, believers in Jesus Christ, nonbelievers in Jesus Christ, and those who are skeptical that God still produces life-saving miracles each and every day. I have resolved to take an active stand in the war for organ donation. Organ transplants are a specialized world of their own in the medical profession. Everything is specialized and every medical professional highly trained, and the end result is a very high rate of success!

I am going through chemotherapy every two weeks as I continue onward toward the completion of my book. Many set-backs have befallen me. I have been knocked down with severe fatigue and just feeling ill, but, I get back up time and time again and trudge forward to get my manuscript to the publisher.

As I walked through my life, step by step, I see how God has had a destiny for me. He has given me the strength to endure all of my medical adversities so I could accomplish His planned purpose. Without the rocky road of medical challenges I would not have grown to become the person I am today. A champion is not afraid of any large adversary. Even though it's been a tough road to walk, I'm glad that I've been tough enough (with God's help) to successfully walk it! Once I mapped out my life I was able to know how to obtain the solution to achieve my goal of being healthy. The miracles that God has blessed me with at exactly the right time will be what I talk about in the following pages.

This book takes the form of both a narrative and an interview. After each chapter's story is told, an interviewer has asked profound and intriguing questions. Many of the interviewer's questions were collected over thirty years and I had never deeply thought about the answers until now. Truthful answers to these profound questions helped me realize I have suppressed a great deal of hurt in the depths of my memory. The hurt that inundated me at the time of the medical challenges had my subconscious suppressing each of the traumatic times in my life. I have purposely reached deep within myself to allow the memories of the beautiful God inspired miracles and also the fantastic medical marvels to come out. Now, everyone can read how incredible they are and could have only come from God!

May this book bring inspiration, education and be a wake up call for anyone not believing that miracles still happen!"

Steven W. Cooke

Chapter One

Before Kidney Failure

⟿

"In 1971 I was a stereotypical freshman at Mariposa County High School in California. My parents had divorced two years earlier. I had a lot of free reign as a teenager, but I did not take advantage of it like most teenagers would have. To me, school was a place to socialize, because living out in the country was very boring. I really enjoyed being with my friends at school. Once I was old enough to drive, my life changed. Now, I had freedom to roam. I owned a black 1957 Chevy Bel-Air hotrod! Now, I could drive to school instead of enduring the dreaded one hour bus ride. I joined the high school wrestling team my sophomore year and really enjoyed the challenge of an adversary. I wrestled my sophomore, junior and senior years in high school.

One day, a friend invited me for an Assembly of God church campout as one of the camp counselors. I thought it would be fun to camp overnight in the woods and be a counselor to a bunch of little kids. What I didn't know was I was going to be saved that night! Around the campfire after the little kids were asleep, all the counselors were singing the traditional camp songs and talking about what we thought of God. Suddenly the Holy Spirit came over us all. Everyone there who was not saved was saved! We all started to weep and accepted Jesus into our hearts. I was saved at 15 years old but could not imagine what this new-found salvation would mean to me in the future.

Even though I had accepted Jesus into my heart, I thought I could keep doing what I was always doing. I was a carnal Christian. I was living the worldly, sinful ways when I was healthy. Once I became ill, I would then turn to God during my time of infirmity and for about a year or so afterwards. I did my share of doing many stupid and self-centered things as most teenagers do! I was a good-hearted teenager, did well in school, and did not cause problems in or out of school.

I enjoyed going to the prom my junior and senior year and attending other dances throughout those years. Shortly after my senior prom, I realized something was not right within me. Physically, I was just slightly off. My energy level was declining, the strength I once had, I did not have any more. I was dizzy much of the time, but I did not see a doctor about the fatigue, dizziness, and shortness of breath I was experiencing. I graduated from high school in

June of 1975 with my kidneys slowly losing their functioning capabilities. I was slowly dying and did not know it!"

Interviewer: Mr. Cooke, have you ever thought how different your life might be if you were not saved and a believer in Jesus Christ and God?

Answer: *"Please drop the formalities and call me Steve. I don't think I would have as much self-confidence as I have. From 15 years old on, when I prayed, I totally expected that prayer to be answered. Prayer gave me an incredible amount of self-confidence that I could literally do anything. Without God, I know I could have never endured the incredible pain, both physically and mentally, that I have endured. When I was in severe pain, I would often think how much pain Jesus had gone through as he was crucified on the cross. I would have died young if God had not saved me from my medical demise. God kept me alive time and time and time again."*

Interviewer: Where has your optimistic attitude come from?

Answer: *"I have always had an optimistic attitude. It is something that I feel I was born with and was reinforced by my biological mother Joyce (Cooke) Moser. The glass has always been half full to me, never half empty. I saw early in life, your attitude makes who and what you are. When a person wakes up in the morning, why would they purposely choose to have a negative attitude and a bad day? It just doesn't make sense to me why some people do that. Life is so much nicer when you choose to be happy and positive. Laughing and a sense of humor is part of my optimistic attitude and I also consider it a form of alternative medicine. Science has proved that patients with an optimistic and humorous attitude have a higher rate of survival and heal much faster than those patients without a positive attitude. Science has also proved patients who pray and are prayed for also have a higher rate of survival and heal faster. Interesting isn't it?"*

Interviewer: Where did you get your never- say-die, never-quit attitude that you have?

Answer: *"It was instilled in me as a child. My mother Joyce (Cooke) Moser, always told me that "I could do anything I put my mind to". First, having a positive attitude taught to me by my mother and knowing that God answers prayer, I figured that I couldn't lose. I was very short as a child and only grew to 5'2" tall. Life seemed to be harder for me due to my short stature. I was always trying hard to overcome various obstacles and keep up with my older brother Mike and the other kids. My father Frank T. Cooke also instilled a lot of toughness in me as I grew up in the country lifestyle. Later in life, being on the varsity wrestling team at Mariposa County*

High School gave me a mindset to have more confidence and also physically toughened me. These early challenges helped me to endure the medical adversities that were ahead of me. Now, I totally rely on God for my strength and healing and my doctors to give me medical advise and appropriate medicine."

Interviewer: Why do you think God has kept you alive?

Answer: *"I really do believe that God has a planned purpose for me. For years, I searched for what I was to do with my life. Everything I thought was a good idea was my idea, not God's, so nothing I tried panned out! God put an idea in my head in 1976, and I never followed through with it. This was the one idea I thought was too big for me and that I could never accomplish.*

In 2005, 29 years later, I was very ill with a bacterial infection in my blood. The doctors at the John C. Fremont Hospital Emergency Room in Mariposa, California, told me many times that they thought they could not save me! The bacterial infection had spread in my bloodstream throughout my body and was seriously affecting my organs. I was placed in a Medi-Flight helicopter. At 2500 feet in the air, the flight nurse told me again that they didn't think that they could save me. I despaired that I never followed through with the idea God gave me in 1976. This was the only regret I had in life. I finally began to do a little here and a little there with His idea.

*A year later, the doctors told me I had a 50/50 chance to live through the cancer I had in my bladder. I got into very deep and intense prayer as I thought I would die from this cancer. I kept thinking of the idea from 1976, and I was saddened that I never completely followed through with it. I asked God what I should do now that I might die in a short amount of time. An overwhelming peaceful sense covered me and went throughout my whole body. All I could think of was His answer, "**GO FORTH AND BE BOLD!**" This hit me hard and ultimately sunk into my hard head! I finally listened and went forth and founded the non-profit HealthQuest House Foundation that offers overnight accommodations and a variety of services for organ transplant patients and their required support personnel for this was His idea of 1976."*

Chapter 2

Kidney Failure

~~~

" After high school, I was working during the summer at a ranch in Mariposa, California. As fall approached, I registered at Merced Community College with a business major. While attending college I was becoming noticeably ill. As my health declined, my breathing became more and more labored. Fatigue set in, and my muscles began to cramp. October rolled around, and it was all I could do just to make it to my classes on time.

On October 5, 1975, after a night of vomiting and continual leg and stomach cramps, I went and saw my local doctor. He diagnosed me with the flu. On my return appointment the next day, my doctor diagnosed me with bronchitis. On my Friday appointment, my doctor diagnosed me with bronchial pneumonia. I was no longer able to sleep lying down. If I tried to lie down to sleep, my lungs sounded like an old fashioned percolator coffeepot. I did not know my lungs were filling with fluids, and

I was literally drowning in my own fluids! To sleep, I sat at the dining room table and laid my head on a pillow.

First thing Monday morning I called and made an immediate appointment. The doctor could see I was in very serious condition. My doctor ordered x-rays, and the x-rays confirmed his thoughts. I had end-stage kidney failure. My doctor told me I needed to get to St. Agnus Medical Center in Fresno, California, as soon as possible! It was a very long ninety mile ride from my mountain community of Mariposa down to Fresno in the valley. My father drove me as I was too sick to drive.

As I was registering at the hospital, I became very dizzy. The next thing I knew, I was being placed on a gurney. I was being wheeled down a very long hallway. Ceiling lights of the hallway were racing by—everything was a blur! I was placed in bed in a room with nurses continually coming in and out. Blood work was taken and chest x-rays were taken. One doctor after another came and saw me. They all asked basic questions and then said they would have to refer me to another doctor. I was very frustrated with their lack of wanting to take me as a patient.

This same scenario went on time and time again. The eighth doctor that came in was the wonderful Dr. Andre Minuth. Dr. Minuth said he was going to take me as his patient. This was a relief to me as I knew I was very sick, the doctors that had been seeing me were not doing anything for me. Dr. Minuth startled me when he told me that my kidneys had failed, and they needed to cut a hole through my stomach to save my life! He said this was called an emergency peritoneal dialysis.

My gown was removed, my stomach scrubbed with Betadine solution, and the doctor told me to grab the bed rails that the nurse had put up. The doctor said he could not use much anesthetic, as I had to flex my stomach muscles and arch my back into the air so he could make a straight incision below my belly button. I grabbed the bed rails tight, I flexed my stomach muscles, and I arched my back. The extreme pain from the cut of the scapel knocked the air out of me!

The doctor said again, "Flex those stomach muscles and arch that back. I need to do to another cut." For the second time, the air was knocked out of me! I could feel my warm blood running down my stomach, crotch and upper legs. The doctor urged me once again to assume the position so he could do another cut. The pain was more than I had ever felt or could imagine! I had my head arched back so I did not have to look at the doctor and the nurses and all the blood!

On my right side near my head was the most kindhearted nurse. As she looked down at me, she told me to take her hand and squeeze her hand for comfort. I did take her hand with my right hand. As the doctor cut once again, I squeezed the hand of this compassionate nurse. I realized that I was very strong and could easily break her hand. I told the nurse I could not squeeze her hand as I would hurt her. She told me, "You can't hurt me." I knew better and released her hand and grabbed the bed rails once again.

I looked up at her and she lovingly grinned down at me. Her lovely smile coupled with her beautiful flowing platinum blond hair did help to divert my attention from the excruciating pain. I continued to grasp the bed rails with each hand and pull them together as my way to get through the pain. Finally, the doctor was done, the painful ordeal was over.

After I was cleaned up and most medical personnel gone, I told one of the few remaining nurses that I would like to thank the nurse that held my hand and comforted me. She said there was not a nurse at my right side holding my hand. They were all at my abdomen area, working intensely on me and assisting the doctor. I insisted on wanting to thank this well-meaning blonde nurse who tried to comfort me. The nurse in my room told me to look to my right. As I looked where I said the blonde nurse was standing and holding my hand, I saw nothing but surgical instrument trays and the night stand with the telephone on it. There absolutely was no room for a nurse to be in that area! Instantly a warm feeling went throughout my body and a smile came to my face. I knew I had held the hand of an angel sent from God!

The peritoneal dialysis put a salt solution into my abdominal cavity, which pulled the fluids out of my lungs. It was then pumped out, this procedure repeated time and time again. After five days of treatment I was transported to San Francisco to go on the hemodialysis unit (kidney machine) as there was not room in the Fresno hemodialysis unit.

In a few weeks a spot opened up back at the Fresno hemodialysis unit and I was able to dialyze there instead of staying in San Francisco at an expensive hotel.

I traveled the ninety mile trek down to Fresno and then ninety miles back home to Mariposa three times a week. For eight months my routine was to leave at 5:30 a.m. to be hooked up to hemodialysis by 7 a.m. After eight hours of cleansing my blood, I was then able to drive myself home again. I really should not have been driving.

I was still sicker than sick! After eight months of dialysis, I was so weak I could barely comb my hair or brush my teeth. At 19 years old, I was ready to die! In my right forearm I had tubes to hook me up to the hemodialysis unit, one tube into a vein and one tube into an artery. Inside my left forearm, I had the vein from a bulls neck surgically connected from an artery to a vein and the high pressure from the artery expanded this vein to a very large size. This procedure is called a bovine fistula. This fistula would soon be used by inserting needles into it instead of using the tubes in my right forearm. These tubes can easily become infected or be accidently pulled out causing a major bleed.

In February, 1976, I had just undergone surgery. I was called to receive a kidney transplant but had to turn it down because of the recent surgery. I was not well enough to undergo a transplant operation. That kidney was not to be mine. With a saddened heart I accepted this fact. I was in a depressed state and needed a kidney badly as I was slowly dying! I kept thinking "God must not want me to have that kidney; He must have another kidney for me."

Every day was an intense struggle to survive. The cramps were awful, my lungs were continually filling with fluids and affecting my breathing. Living in the Sierra Nevada mountains in the winter, we have deep snow. I had to put snow chains on my vehicle while I was so sick that my muscles were cramping and I was physically spent and then drive ninety miles to the dialysis center. This ordeal took every ounce of strength I could muster. About halfway there, I had to take the snow chains off as I got down to the lower elevation and the roads were not icy or snow covered. By the time I arrived at the dialysis center I was wet, cold, and totally exhausted!

From October, 1975, to June 14, 1976, I was on hemodialysis. It was not working well for me. At 19 years of age I was resigned to dying! I made plans to fly back to Michigan and see all of my relatives, then come home and die. I had my trip scheduled and was looking forward to seeing my cousins. The final time for me to be on hemodialysis was June 14, 1976 then fly back to Michigan. It was on that day, when I arrived at the hemodialysis unit, the head nurse told me, "They have a kidney for you Steven." I was so set on dying that I did not want the kidney transplant that would save my life. It took about thirty minutes of serious thought and a lot of convincing by the head nurse for me to make my decision to receive the kidney transplant."

Interviewer: Do you feel like a ball that always bounces back?

Answer: *"Yeah, now I do. When I was younger, I thought I could survive any medical challenge thrown at me. As I have aged and become wiser, I realize that God has a plan for me and until I complete His plan, I will always bounce back. There is not any medical reason why I am still alive, just a Heavenly one."*

Interviewer: Have you ever asked, "Why me?"

Answer: *"As I think back, I can never think of a time that I said, "Why me?" Now I can see that God was molding and developing me to become what He wanted me to be so I can complete His planned purpose in my life. At different times, when I have been in the hospital, I have heard patients complaining about their ailments and saying,"Why me"? I have decided not to have PMS but to have PMA (positive mental attitude). As we walk down the path of our life, we will probably stumble and fall. It's not about if you will fall, it's about your attitude when you hit the ground and how fast you pick yourself up. In life, many of us will take two steps forward and then one step backwards. This is alright because you are still going forward. You see, our lives are not determined by what happens to us, but, it is how we react to what happened to us. One of the main things our lives are all about is the attitude we bring into various situations. If you have a positive attitude it will cause a chain reaction of positive thoughts and positive outcomes. A positive attitude will be a catalyst...a spark that creates extraordinary results. Those that realize that the Holy Bible tells us how to be a positive person in a negative situation have a distinct advantage on those who don't understand the wisdom that the Holy Bible holds and what Jesus Christ did for us."*

Interviewer: How did you come up with the title of this book?

Answer: *"For many years I wanted to do this book, I procrastinated and just talked about writing my book. The only step I took towards doing this book was to have the title, 'Twice Transplanted'. One day while I was in prayer, I asked God what I should name my book. Immediately, what I should name my book came to me as an overwhelming thought: 'Conversations with a Masterpiece, Miracles and Medical Marvels'. As I thought about renaming my book, I realized that the doctors in San Francisco at the trans-*

plant centers refer to me as their masterpiece. They call me this because many, many surgeons have all dedicated a few strokes of their scapel to me to make me their masterpiece of work."

Interviewer: Do you faint at the sight of blood?

Answer: *"I was very sensitive to the sight of blood. Still today, I cannot watch them stick me with a needle. As I have aged and seen so much blood and suffering, I don't have a problem with the sight of blood or watching surgeries."*

Interviewer: Are you afraid of needles?

Answer: *"That's a hard question. I would say, "Yes, I am afraid of needles," as I know needles and pain go hand in hand, and no one likes pain. I also know that needles deliver the required medicine to help us regain our health."*

Interviewer: Do you think the angel was ethereal?

Answer: *"Yes, I do believe that the lovely nurse was an angel sent from Heaven at exactly the perfect time to comfort me in my time of need."*

Chapter 3

Kidney Transplant

~~~

"My dad, Frank T. Cooke, drove me to the University of California San Francisco, Moffitt Hospital for my kidney transplant. I was left in my room to contemplate the upcoming life-saving surgery. I was nervous and hesitant at what was awaiting me. I had to endure the upcoming surgery or die! At 10:30 p.m. they rolled me into the operating room. At 6:00 a.m. they rolled me out! When I awoke, my world that I had known had changed.

I had a twelve inch incision through my left abdomen and a catheter into my bladder, which seemed the size of a garden hose! Even though I really hurt bad from the surgery, I felt much healthier as my new kidney was working well. During the eight days I was catheterized, I watched chunks of tissue and clotted blood flow through the catheter tube and into a bag! I was quickly turned into an adult patient who had life-saving major surgery and all that went with it.

The nurses at UCSF were great! They were very caring and attentive. The nurses really were concerned about their patients. Most of the nurses seem to have been from the midwest. The U.S. Olympic team was competing in the 1976 Olympics, and the nurses knew most of the competitors. It was nice to interact with them as they told real-life experiences with the athletes I was seeing on TV. By July 4th I was feeling quite a bit better. I was walking around the hospital halls and rarely in my bed. My friend Larry and I met in the hospital, we both received a kidney transplant. The nurse told my friend Larry and I that we could get an outside pass to take the bus around the city. We got the outside pass...what a mistake!

As we rode the bus around the city, at twelve noon about five blocks from the medical center, the bus stopped and the driver said, "All out"! The bus system was to shut down at 12 noon on the Fourth of July. My friend and I could barely make it up the steps in and out of the bus. How were we to walk five blocks up very steep streets to the medical center?

We finally made it after many stops along the way. Being on diuretics and no restrooms available to speak of, I embarrassingly admit we watered the few trees we could find. After this outing, I became very ill with bacterial infections. I was again constantly in bed, very tired, sore, with a fever, and my new kidney transplant was rejecting! July turned into August and I was once again dying! My white blood cell count had dropped dangerously low. I was placed in reverse isolation, anyone who came into my room had to gown up and put on a mask. I wasted away from 160 pounds to a mere 114 pounds as the bacterial infection consumed me.

The team of doctors stood around my bed and advised me that they must remove my new kidney transplant, it was literally killing me! I knew, if they removed it and I went back on hemodialysis, I would soon die. I struck a deal with the doctors. If my white blood cells remained at the same level or were higher the next day, they would leave the kidney transplant in.

I started to pray, and I prayed and I prayed and I prayed. The day turned into night, the night into early morning. I looked at the clock, it was 4:30 a.m. In an incredibly peaceful and diligent prayer, I fell into a warm and fuzzy place where I was on a higher level with my God. I knew my life would soon be over if they removed my kidney transplant, so I gave my kidney transplant, all my medical issues and all that I was to God. I finally surrendered. I knew I could not handle the pain anymore, nor the anguish and the torments I was going through.

As I gave it all to God, Jesus appeared to me at the foot of my bed. I slowly opened my eyes and saw the upper torso of Jesus hanging on the cross. His chin was down on his chest and his arms were nailed outward on the cross. Jesus slowly raised

His head, looked at me, and a grin came upon his face. An all enveloping warm sense of peace came over me! All I could feel and sense was, "It will be all right." With this incredible peace about me, I quickly fell asleep.

When I awoke it was 10 a.m. and the team of doctors was standing around me. My doctors told me, "We have to take your blood again. There must have been a mistake." I told them, "They haven't taken my blood yet." The doctors told me, "Your blood was taken at 5:30 a.m. You must have slept through it, we have the results back. We were expecting your white blood cells to have dropped. Your white blood cells for the first time have remained at the exact same level." I told them to remember our deal, "If my white blood cells are at the same level or raised up, you leave my kidney transplant in."

The doctors agreed to take another blood test and see if the results came back the same. The results were the same, so my transplant was left in! I was so happy that I was turning the corner on my bad health. By Saturday my white blood cells had risen considerably! I do believe Jesus stepped in and touched me with a miraculous healing! A few days later, on Thursday morning, my mother, Joyce (Cooke) Moser, came and picked me up. They were required to take me by wheelchair to the front door of the hospital. I boldly and proudly walked out of the medical center almost two months after I walked in, as a soft breeze blew against my cheek I knew that Jesus was directly instrumental in my successful kidney transplant!

Once home, an overwhelming desire to build a sailboat and sail off into the sunset was all I thoought about. I wondered if my kidney transplant came from a sailor who met his/her fate at sea. I did not want to buy a sailboat, I wanted to build one from scratch. It seemed I had bought every book there was on how to build a 40 foot sloop. While I was educating myself on how to build my sailboat, I bought a 12 foot catamaran to sail on the lakes near me. I never did build my 40 foot sloop. The desire went away within a year year.

As I healed, I was required to take a myriad of medicines for the rest of my life. The main anti-rejection drug I was required to take for my kidney transplant was named Prednisone. Prednisone is a steroid and it can give many serious short term and long term side effects. A nurse once told me "If you live twenty-five years you will hate your body." As I slowly felt better and better, I had a great desire to go to church after having such a religious experience.

I attended The Little Church in the Hills in Mariposa, California, which is a non-denomi-national church. After my experiences with my wonderful angel and then Jesus hanging on the cross, my spiritual views had definitely changed. Even though I accepted Jesus as my savior when I was 15 years old, I thought that's all there was to being a Christian. I made many friends at The Little

Church in the Hills. Many of these friends are still my in my life. Many of us have moved far away from each other, but we still keep in contact and manage to have lunch together now and again."

Interviewer: How can you be so brave?

Answer: *"I don't think it is anything about being brave. It is that I simply do what I need to do to survive. If I don't get stuck with needles or have the required surgeries, I will die. I don't want to die, so I go through the surgeries with an optimistic attitude. I try to focus on the things I can control and let God have the rest. One advantage I have over most people is that I have figured out the importance of living and dying and by figuring that out I know the importance of how to live a life worth living."*

Interviewer: Do you have nightmares about the suffering you have gone through?

Answer: *"In the beginning I use to have some pretty bad ones. Now, I don't have any nightmares. I was tired of having them and I asked God to take them away, and He did. Now, I have great dreams! My dreams are in full color, with sound and have many of my former classmates in them. I just love my dreams."*

Interviewer: Have you suffered from Post Traumatic Stress Syndrome?

Answer: *"I did have many challenges with Post Traumatic Stress Syndrome. It came later on as I had more and more surgeries. I read about it to understand it. Then I did what I always do, I prayed for it to be taken away from me. I adjusted, adapted and overcame it. It was a long process. I spoke with my doctor about it, I educated myself about it and I prayed about it. It was about a year before I felt like my Post Traumatic Stress Syndrome challenges were over. Not all prayers are answered instantly."*

Interviewer: Have you ever passed out due to the severe pain?

Answer: *"No, but there has been many times that I wished I could have, so I would not have felt the excruciating pain. Many times I thought I would faint, but I didn't."*

Interviewer: Can you disassociate yourself from pain?

Answer: *"Unfortunately I cannot disassociate myself from the pain. I have heard of people who can put themselves into another place where they do not feel pain. What I do is I pray while the intense pain is happening and that helps to put me in a much more tranquil place so I don't notice the pain as much. Humor is also essential in my life. I joke around a lot and act a little crazy so I won't go insane with the seriousness of my medical issues."*

Chapter 4

Hip Replacements

⌒‿

"The steroid medicine I was required to take so my kidney transplant would not reject was suddenly taking its toll. A side-effect of the steroids is that it reduces the blood flow to the hip sockets. After being starved for blood, my hip socket literally died and started to collapse! Walking became very difficult, just moving was extremely painful! Within three years the high levels of steroids had caused serious damage to my joints, especially my hips. I needed to have both of my hips replaced with steel and plastic.

In October, 1979, I was back at UCSF Moffitt Hospital to have both hips replaced during one admittance. This is the type of surgery a person usually has when they become elderly, not when they're 22 years old! The doctors decided to replace my right hip first. When I awoke, my right leg was completely out to the side and my foot was up near my right shoulder! I could scratch my big toe without bending. It took eight days to get my leg back to straight ahead of me and then down to resting on the bed. After a few days of being up on crutches, the decision was made to replace my left hip socket.

My first hip surgery went well, my second hip surgery was quite a challenge. I woke up as they were wheeling me out of the operating room, my body convulsing and trembling. In the recovery room I had extreme difficulties breathing and coming out of the anesthesia. The recovery room was very traumatic and life altering for me!

Lying in the hospital bed that I was put on after surgery, I was being wheeled up to my room with my left leg suspended out to the side. From the recovery room I was taken into the elevator. When we arrived at my floor the elevator door opened, the elevator floor was slightly lower than the hospital floor. The orderly had problems getting my bed all the way out of the elevator. The elevator door started to close and pushed my left leg inward to the bed frame. Fresh out of surgery the extreme pain that overcame me was unbelievable!

The pain from this elevator experience never did leave. It was incredible pain day and night, night and day! Morphine did not seem to work, the pain did not leave. The doctors did not know why I had such pain. The x-rays showed everything was fine. Each day the physical therapist would try to slowly get my leg back toward centerline, it was not working. The continual pain I was in was driving me insane, it never stopped! After eight days I could not take it anymore. I wanted to die so the pain would stop! Praying was all that was left, nothing else was working. Because I could not sleep, I prayed into the night, prayer after prayer after prayer for God to please stop the pain.

The night turned into early morning. As I was at the end of my rope, I could take no more. I surrendered my total self-being and gave my whole body to Jesus Christ. At the end of the prayer, I opened my eyes. At the foot of my bed I saw the upper portion of Jesus on the cross once again! The arms of Jesus were spread wide and nailed to the cross. Once again, He raised His chin from His chest and looked at me with a compassionate grin. An overwhelming warm fuzzy sensation of "It's going to be all right." enveloped me. I quickly fell asleep. When I awoke the next morning the Physical Therapist easily brought my leg over to centerline and down to the bed without much pain at all!

A few days later I was wheeled to the front door and I walked out on crutches. These two surgeries I had endured were so severe, it took me three and a half months to learn how to walk again! My legs kept wanting to go outward instead of forward and backwards. During a check-up to see how my hips were doing, my doctor noticed my eyes were yellow. I was jaundiced! A blood test revealed that I had Hepatitis B and that is the reason I was jaundiced. I was never told that Hepatitis B is a life threatening virus and the consequences of Hepatitis B is liver failure.

Interviewer: Does it bother you to take pills everyday?

Answer: *"No, not at all. I have been taking pills my entire life. I don't know what it is like to not take pills daily. Many people take a lot more vitamins and minerals than I take with my required medicine."*

Interviewer: Have you ever been healthy in your adult life?

Answer: *"Sure, after my kidney transplant I had three years of feeling great before I needed my hips replaced. After the hip replacements I had 15 years of carefree, pain free living. I was married for nineteen years and have two beautiful children, Stacey and David."*

Interviewer: Do you blame God for your ill health?

Answer: *"No, not at all! God is my Father in Heaven. Just as your father here on earth only wants the best for us, so does He. That is why He sent angels in my time of need to comfort me by holding my hand to defeat the demons Satan sent and had Jesus appear twice at the foot of my bed when I needed Him. I blame Satan, who has attacked me with infirmities and tried to destroy me before I can fulfill my planned purpose that God has for me. As far as I'm concerned, behind every scar I have, there is an incredible story of how Jesus Christ came to my rescue."*

Interviewer: Why do you think all of your medical adversities have happened to you?

Answer: *"Well, I'm an observer. I observe the people around me. I notice how they act and what they say and do. My mind is always working, and I take these observations and try to grow and develop myself into a better person by what I have seen and heard. With every medical challenge, I grow to be a better person. Each one of my afflictions I consider as a test. When I endure these tests, I have a __test__imony to share! Without a test, I cannot have a __test__imony. I feel I am chosen by God to give my testimony to the world, this is one reason why I am writing this book.*

A very famous evangelist once told my parents that "I would do great things one day." Years ago, after this evangelist had told my parents what he did about me, I did not believe I had greatness in me. There was a short time in my life where I was not self-confident and I did not have self-esteem about what I could really do if I wanted to. I am only 5 foot, 2 inches and have multiple medical problems, what great thing could I do? After many years of educating myself in what the Bible says, I have matured and know that all things are possible through God. Matthew 19:26 says: "But Jesus looked at them and said to them, **With men this is impossible, but with God all things are possible.***" Now, I definitely know that I have greatness within me, I am finally letting it develop and flow out of me. This book and my non-profit HeathQuest House Foundation are two of the ways I am letting my greatness out.*

I have also learned to be a giver. I love to give, whether it be letting someone in the grocery line with just a few items ahead of me or helping someone with a ride across town. When I am in the hospital, I try to have some of the medical personnel I am around take something positive from me even though I am the patient. Medical personnel are use to cranky patients with short tempers. When I arrive, I arrive bearing dark chocolate for all the nurses. This little bit of sweets will benefit the patient a hundred fold and make you a new friend that is easy to talk to. These medical adversities have also given me the chance for me to sell you my book! Did I tell you I have a sense of humor?"

Chapter 5

Before Liver Transplant

⟨~~~⟩

"As the years went by, my health was relatively good and I got married and we had two beautiful children, Stacey and David. My kidney transplant was working great! My hip replacements were not hurting and also worked very well. To me, it seemed like I never had any medical problems. The doctors had really accomplished a great job at giving me back my health. God gave me the ability to quickly leave my problems and challenges of yesterday behind me, just like water rolling off a duck's back. I did my routine blood tests and medical checkups every month. Other than taking pills everyday, you would never have known where I had been in the marvelous medical world.

In 1994, I once again noticed how my strength was starting to diminish. Fatigue was slowly setting in. I seemed to live in a whirlwind of confusion, making good sound decisions was very difficult for me. Over the years my doctors had kept an eye on my blood work. My doctor told me that my liver was slowing down. At one of my appointments my doctor told me, "I think you are going to need a liver transplant." It hit me so hard, so suddenly, I went into shock and almost passed out after hearing those awful words. It devastated me, it took me a half hour to be able to physically get up and off the exam table at the doctor's office!

Now, I had a reason as to why I was becoming so confused and fatigued! The Hepatitis B virus had destroyed my liver and I needed a liver transplant or I would die! I had been in the organ transplant world, I did not want to be there again. At first I resigned to die rather than go through the long ordeal of a liver transplant. Once I regained my senses, I knew I had a family to live for.

This was a whole different world than the kidney transplant world. With the kidney transplant in 1976, I was automatically placed on the transplant list. With kidney failure, there is the kidney machine to keep you alive until you receive a kidney transplant. There is not a liver machine to keep you alive until you receive a liver transplant. Obtaining a liver transplant in 1997 was quite different. There was a great mountain to climb just to get on the liver transplant list! Three thousand dollars was required so my support person and I could live in the big city near the organ transplant medical center for up to 30 days after the transplant.

I did not have three thousand dollars so I started various fund-raising campaigns. I live in Paradise, California, a beautiful community in the tall pines just 90 miles north of Sacramento. We had car washes and put out cash collection containers at restaurants and food stores. My parents Frank and Betty Cooke of Mariposa, California gave me an incredible start with one thousand dollars! Regrettably, I was not attending church at this time of my life.

I went to a church here in Paradise, California to ask them if they had some youths who could volunteer to help with the car washes to assist me in raising funds. This loving church did not know me, I did not attend their church, but they gave me a very large sum of money to help me meet the three thousand dollar requirement! I'm not going to name this wonderful church as I don't want anyone to try to take advantage of their generosity. God certainly gave me uncommon favor with this sensational church. By all rights, they should not have contributed the amount they did. This was the only church I asked for help from and they blessed so much more than I ever imagined possible.

The lovely people of my wonderful community of Paradise, California also gave so much from their hearts and I reached my three thousand dollar goal with their generosity. I was astounded at how much they supported me. Now, from the bottom of my heart, I try to give back a small portion of the generosity they gave me. The cash collection containers at store check-out stands had a photo of me on it with a short explanation of why I needed their financial donations, they came through with flying colors! The people of Paradise, California helped me to regain my faith in the goodness of my fellow man.

I was also required to attend Alcoholic Anonymous meetings twice a week even though I did not drink alcohol anymore. I quit drinking beer and white wine coolers on March 10, 1996, and now five months later in August, 1996, I am required by my insurance company to attend AA meetings. Being as sick as I was, I hated attending the AA meetings. Now, I can see it helped me to understand more about the difficulties an alcoholic goes through. I have much more compassion for those who need to attend the AA meetings to defeat this horrible disease.

A misdirected letter of organ transplant denial came to me from my insurance company. This letter seemed to be the straw that broke the camel's back for my already struggling marriage. This letter was to have been delivered to the Liver Transplant Services at California Pacific Medical Center, Pacific Campus in San Francisco, California. As my health quickly declined, my divorce was imminent and happening at the worst time I could ever imagine."

Interviewer: Do you feel alone when you are all alone in the hospital?

Answer: *"I have felt alone in the hospital when I was younger. Now, after many surgeries, I never feel alone. I have Jesus Christ in my heart, and He gives me all the company I need. I did miss my children immensely. My Stacey and David were out of my life for quite along time. My good friend, Michael Decker, has really supported me. When I go in the hospital in San Francisco, he stays at a local hotel and visits me every day. He has become more than just a friend, he has become a loving brother to me."*

Interviewer: What are a couple of things you miss doing that you used to be able to do?

Answer: *"Probably running is the thing I miss most. When my daughter Stacey was learning to ride a bike and fly a kite and I could not run with her, it greatly saddened me. I also miss doing laborious outside work. I like getting dirty, working in the yard trimming bushes, landscaping and things like painting a house. All of these things I cannot do any more."*

Interviewer: Do you feel you were cheated out of life because of your physical ailments?

Answer: *"No I don't. I have had a great life! I have had a full life! My life may not have been what people consider a normal life. I have experienced so very much more than the average person can ever imagine. Physically and psychologically, my life has been different. Physically, I cannot do some things, but I can do most things to get by in life. Psychologically, I have seen the full scale of challenges and have managed to maintain a positive attitude. I think when you get up in the morning, it's your decision to have a good happy day or have a bad rotten day. I always choose to have a good happy day with God's blessings. Proverbs 23:7 So a man thinkith so is he"*

Interviewer: Does it bother you to continually have serious medical challenges?

Answer: *"It does bother me somewhat to have one serious medical challenge after another. Since 1997, as soon as I have gotten over one medical challenge, another one comes up. It does get very tiresome and wears on my emotions. For awhile I felt like all of my emotions had been used up, I couldn't cry or have compassion for people. Now, it is just the opposite. I feel God has displayed His glory in my trials and tremendous victories. It has given me a different perspective on life. I see most people live as if death is at a far distance. I think we should live as if death is eminent within a year, yet, have wisdom and discernment with our finances as if we will live a long life. When you know how to die, then you will know how to really live your life to the fullest!"*

Interviewer: What do you do to keep your reservoir of hope and love alive?

Answer: *"I try to get closer to God. I listen to Christian music in the day and pray many times during the day. When I go to bed, I play a cassette tape or CD of a Christian pastor's sermon. This way I end the day listening to the word of God. I find when I wake up, I am much happier than I would be if I did not listen to God's word the night before. The Holy Bible says in Proverbs 23:7 "So a man thinkith so is he." I remind myself of this continually during the day and do my best to live it by thinking of the good positive things and not the bad negative things."*

Chapter 6

Liver Transplant

~~~

I was in the hospital most of the summer of 1997. In mid August I was released since I was doing better, but by October I was once again seriously ill. On October 2, 1997, I was scheduled to be readmitted and told, "You will not walk out of this medical center without a liver transplant." What they were saying was, "You are going to die or receive your liver transplant this time in the hospital."

With the mental confusion that end-stage liver failure causes, I was really struggling to make sense of it all. I needed a ride to California Pacific Medical Center in San Francisco, California, on October 2nd. It is about a 200 mile trip from Paradise, California. Everyone I asked seemed to have a reason why they could not take me. Being very independent and resourceful, I called up the Greyhound bus lines, packed my bag, bought a ticket and was on my way to San Francisco for my life-saving liver transplant!

In the hospital, the days dragged on and on. Every day seemed like week. Being as sick as I was, in the pain I was in and having the confusion due to the illness was pure torture! I was not the only one awaiting a liver transplant. I met some wonderful people also in the twilight of their lives. Two bits of shining lights were named Bill Lynn and Carol Ann Averil. They were both awaiting liver transplants as I was. We morbidly joked with each other, "You're going to die before I do." We would see the nightly news and wonder if a liver transplant for us would come from one of the car accidents we saw on that newscast. Liver failure causes day night reversal. You want to sleep during the day and are awake all night. The doctors wanted us to keep up as much of our strength as possible by walking. All night long we would walk the quiet long halls of California Pacific Medical Center. We looked like scary ghouls in the night with yellow skin, massive muscle loss, protruding bones, sunken eyes and with engorged pregnant like bellies stretched out to their maximum limits! What a sight we were.

Bill Lynn had his 13-year-old daughter April, wife Jean and mother Gertrude as his support personnel. At 13 years old, little April stole the hearts of everyone at the transplant center! She was the brightest of the bright lights that shown during that long summer and fall. Her never-ending smile, beautiful white teeth and big brown eyes were always welcomed.

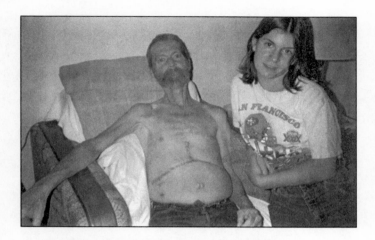

My step-mother, Betty Cooke, was my support person and during this hectic ordeal, she rose up through the stress of it all and became my mother. She went compassionately far beyond what a step-mother is usually considered to be.

On the evening of October 11th, the transplant surgeon came into my room. Transplant surgeons do not take their valuable time to come in your room unless something big is happening. *"They must have a liver for me. They must have a liver for me. I'm not going to die"*, is what I thought! With great expectation I asked "Do you have a liver for me?" With a slow reply he helplessly looked at me and said "Do you have your affairs in order, Mr. Cooke?" It was devastating news that they did not have a liver for me, and the next one was not expected to be received until a few weeks. I only had a few days to live. I would die before a liver was available for me!

For that evening of October 11th and all the next day of October 12th, I was very depressed and tried to accept that I would soon die. Despite all their medical technology and medicines, the doctors and nurses had to sit back and watch me slowly die because they did not have a liver to give to me. Bill Lynn and Carol Ann Averil had just received their livers and now it was a waiting game. Would I survive long enough for another liver to be allocated? Would someone be other-center and say "YES" to organ donation?

I was too tired to pray, I was too sick to care anymore. I conceded to death and just laid in my hospital bed, curled up in a fetal position, not able to eat or drink and waited to succumb to liver failure! I knew where I was with God and that I was going to Heaven. I was not afraid of dying. I was frustrated and disgusted that in this day and age of advanced medicine, I would have to be let die. The next evening; the transplant surgeon came into my room again. What worse news could he give me? I expected some sort of apology that the medical center and their transplant team would have to let me die. I was so wrong! Standing at the foot of my bed, the transplant surgeon said those wonderful words, "*I think we have a liver for you.*" Then he said, "A high school football player was shot in the head gangland style. We are not certain, but it looks very good that you will be getting his liver." I was so thankful. I cannot explain to you how my depression instantly went away. If I had enough energy, I would have cried with joy that I would not die. As I felt joy, I thought about the extreme sadness and tragedy the family of the young man who just died was going through. I said a prayer of comfort for them in their trying times. I also said a prayer of thanks to God for saving me once again.

At 7:00am the next morning I was wheeled into surgery. I was getting my liver transplant and I would not die! The surgery went well and it took six and a half hours to complete. Betty Cooke, my mother, had the hardest job, the job of waiting, worrying and praying for me. I woke up and instantly was happy that I was still alive. I was on a ventilator that was breathing for me. I quickly realized that there was a problem...I was not getting air properly! I could hardly breathe even though I was on the ventilator. I remembered how my awesome nurse coordinator, Karen Devaney, R.N., M.S.N. told me to breathe with the ventilator, so it would work easier. I tried and tried to breathe in sync with the ventilator, but it just wasn't working for me. I blew out air and inhaled air as hard as I physically could. It seemed as if I was trying to breathe through a very skinny drinking straw! With the amount of muscle relaxants I had in me from surgery, I could not raise my hand or move anything to let the nurse know I was in extreme trouble.

The only thing I could move was to stick my tongue out a little bit. I tried to signal the nurse this way. Each and every breath was a huge struggle that took all the strength I had. There was a problem with my diaphragm muscle, this is the muscle that makes you breathe. My diaphragm seemed to be pretty much paralyzed in a middle inhalation state. The ventilator would only pump air into my lungs until they expanded and hit the diaphragm, which then stopped my lungs from expanding by the diaphragm pulling them downwards. I was getting a little more than half of the oxygen content we all need to survive. After many hours of panic and using every ounce of strength I had to breathe, it finally got easier. The muscle relaxants slowly wore off and I could finally breathe like normally.

The next day I was rolled on my side so an intravenous (I.V.) main line could be removed from the side of my neck. I was rolled back onto my back and taken to another room as I was doing much better. After I arrived at my new room, I looked down at the drain tube which was placed in me during surgery for excess blood that may accumulate around the liver. Thick red blood was pouring out of it into the reservoir bulb. The blood loss was calculated at a rate of 2 liters per hour! Two liters is the amount in a large soda bottle! I needed to go back into surgery as soon as possible to stop the suspected bleeder.

I refused to go back into surgery and have those horrible breathing problems again. I was too weak from many hours of struggling to breathe and just could not do it again. I was so affected by not being able to correctly breathe that I would rather die than go back into surgery. Everyone wanted me to have the surgery, even all the surgeons spoke with me. Everyone talked with me and tried to convince me to have the surgery. The Chaplain came in my room, then my mom and April Lynn. The Chaplain said she wanted to pray for me to have the surgery. We all held hands and the Chaplain prayed. As we were about finished with the prayer, I looked up. April Lynn had her eyes open, looking at me, huge tears rolling down her cheeks. I was overwhelmed with a warm enveloping peace, above and beyond what most people could ever understand. For some reason, I instantly connected with the adorable April Lynn. The thought that totally overcame me was, *"This beautiful young person is what life is all about."*

One doctor that seemed extremely nice and had a great bedside manner was the next doctor to speak with me. I told him I would have the surgery if he could guarantee me that I would instantly wake up with full function of my muscles and not be on a ventilator. He agreed to my demands and when I woke up, he was standing at my bedside making sure everything was going perfect.

Before the surgery, I jokingly told my doctor that I would send him a Christmas card if everything went perfect. My doctor did receive his Christmas card. April Lynn also received a Christmas card and a gift as I saw her as saving my life. Only family members over 16 years old were permitted in the room I was in. April Lynn was only 13 years old and not a relative. I think God had a hand at getting her into my room. They are very strict with rules in that part of the hospital as all patients are in critical condition. If she was not in my room, I would have said no to the surgery and probably died! I have a love for April Lynn as I have a love for the entire Holguin family who donated their daughter's liver to me. Anita Maria Holguin was in a horrible car accident, yet she is alive and well within me and I am doing the best I can to carry on her legacy. They were all very instrumental in saving my life. As I reach deep down inside of me and bring up these old memories, I well up with emotions for these wonderful people.

After going through my liver transplant, I definitely was a different man. My relationship with God changed. I had thought you only think about church on Sunday for an hour or so. This is the way

I was raised. Since I was a child, my family always said grace and asked God for His blessing on our food. Other than a mealtime blessing and an hour on Sunday at church, when we did go, we did not do anything religious. I now am quite a different man than I used to be. I started to seek God and His ways. Nobody is a picture-perfect poster child for Christ, nor am I. Daily, I am trying hard to develop myself into a more mature Christian. Now, I am the most contented man I could ever be as I strive to be all God has for me."

Interviewer: Will you have to take anti-rejection medications for the rest of your life?

Answer: *"Yes, I will have to take pills the rest of my life. To me, taking a few pills is nothing. I have taken pills all my life, and it is not very much requested of me to keep my life-saving organ transplants properly functioning. After all I went through to get my organ transplants, I wouldn't want anything to ever happen to it. Also, I feel an obligation to my donor family to do all that I can to keep their loved one's organ that I received as healthy as possible."*

Interviewer: Have you made many friends in the hospital?

Answer: *"Yes, I have made some very good friends. A man named Larry and I were friends when I went through my kidney transplant. Bill Lynn and Carol Ann Averil are wonderful people, they became very good friends to me during and after my liver transplant. I have visited both Bill at his house in Willits, California and Carol Ann at her sister and brother-in-laws house in Los Gatos, California. Carol Ann's brother-in-law, James McIlvain has been awesome to me. James always welcomes me with open arms, a spectacular dinner and then to stay overnight, time and time again.*

Gordie and Lynn Varney of Mariposa, California are great friends that I have known for many years and they have over the years called many hundreds of times to see how I was doing when I was in and out of the hospital. Those daily phone calls kept me going and in touch with the outside world and reminded me that there is my normal life awaiting me as soon as I get healthy enough."

Interviewer: Have you ever felt like giving up and just dying?

Answer: *"Yes, once I have. After my liver transplant surgery, I was in extreme pain and in a very bad state of mind. I just wanted to die! God placed April Lynn in my ICU room so I would change my mind and have the life-saving surgery. I will always have a sincere love in my heart for April."*

Interviewer: Why do you think all these medical challenges have happened to you?

Answer: *"There is not any medical reason I am still alive, just a Heavenly one. God has molded and made me into the man He wanted to fulfill His planned purpose. Without all the trials I have gone through, I would not have the wisdom and discernment that I have about life. His destiny for me is an awesome one that I could have never imagined!"*

Interviewer: Have you experienced different feelings after your transplant like food cravings that you never had?

Answer: *"Yes, with my kidney transplant in 1976, I experienced a great desire to build a sailboat and sail off into the sunset by myself. I did not want to buy a sailboat, I wanted to build it from scratch. I have lived in the mountains most of my life. A sailboat and the ocean life was totally foreign to me.*

After receiving my liver transplant 1997, chocolate was essential for me to be snacking on, and ice cream was always in my freezer. Live music also became very intriguing to me and I wanted to be in a band. I knew nothing about music. I could not read music and I could not play music. Both of these yearnings I never had before my liver transplant. I ended up learning how to run the sound mixer and was a soundman in two bands. I have heard of transplant patients who have many new feelings and desires that they never had before their transplant. I did some research into this subject and bought a book that explains what happens to the human body when it receives an organ transplant. It all has to do with memory cells. The organ that is transplanted into the new human body carries millions of memory cells. Until those memory cells die off and are replaced by the memory cells of the new human body it is in, cravings and desires will happen to the organ transplant recipient. After speaking with various organ transplant recipients, I found that the cravings usually last about six months."

Interviewer: Do you fear death?

Answer: *"Not at all. I have been at death's doorstep so many times that I have become immune to what most people fear. I believe when I die I will go to Heaven. I also believe God will keep me alive until His planned purpose in my life has been fulfilled. I know now that I am doing His planned purpose for me. His planned purpose, I feel, is completing this book so people may be inspired to get through their medical adversity and understand that miracles still do happen. I feel His other purpose for me is to build up the non-profit Christian based HealthQuest House Foundation for organ transplant patients."*

Interviewer: What are some of the things you do to have a successful surgery and regain your health?

Answer: *"Besides prayer, I insist on managing my health with my support person. I use 3 inch by 5 inch cards with questions on the front to ask my doctor and then my support person writes their answer on the back. I feel my health is my responsibility, not my doctors. Having terrific friends and relatives that call daily as Lynn Varney and my cousin Connie Kinnee of Jeddo, Michigan does, really did help me to regain my health both physically and especially emotionally. Friends I have known since I was seven years old like Darlene Benson of Mariposa, California, who sent get well cards at the exact perfect time are also a blessing for me to have. Receiving some mail while in the hospital is a high point and is terrific for the emotional health of a patient."*

Chapter 7

Other Medical Adversities

~~~

"With a new outlook at life, I was a changed man! I enjoyed going to church and all the new friends I made there. With the fire of my life burning hot, I am continually purified to be more like Christ! The fire I went through refined me and made me more able to see His divine planned purpose in life. I grew and grew in my walk with Christ. Over these years of going through various surgeries, I developed into a much more mature Christian. As I matured, I also became a much happier man.

I enjoyed attending a local organ transplant support group in Chico, California. The name of this group is the Northern California Organ Transplant Support Group. I was hesitant to attend an organ transplant support group. I thought support groups were all conducted by social workers who did not understand the transplant patient as they did not receive an organ transplant, their expertise came from book learning. I found out the local transplant support group was run by other transplant recipients, this elated me.

The Northern California Organ Transplant Support Group supports pre-transplant patients as well as post-transplant recipients. Their support includes raising money and doing organ donor awareness presentations. Marjorie Davis, M.S.W. was the social worker overseeing the California Pacific Medical Center, Pacific Campus in San Francisco liver transplant support group. She did an absolutely great job with the support group there and put me at ease. I believe book learning is fine, but I also believe walking a mile in a man's shoes is so much more valuable and develops a compassion that can only be obtained when you survive the long ordeal of an organ transplant. Once a patient receives an organ transplant, they will be different due to what they have experienced and where they have been. They will probably take the time to stop and smell the lovely flowers or give their place in line to a stranger. Before transplant they would not have taken that small amount of time to make their life and their community better.

My heart soon had a major problem! I was under a lot of stress with my medical issues and my divorce was weighing heavy on my heart. Just six months after my liver transplant I was now having heart problems. Several times classic heart attack symptoms hit me. Now, a very severe pain came from my back between my spine and left shoulder blade. I was cold and clammy. Sweat poured off me, I was nauseated and dizzy. I almost fainted and I had trouble breathing. I went to the local hospital and they checked me for a heart attack. All tests came back fine. The tests showed that it was not a heart attack. My cardiac enzymes were fine. This scenario happened time and time again. After about eight to ten of these episodes, I finally had a very bad heart attack. I knew it was definitely a bad heart attack! When I got to the emergency room of the local hospital and had tests conducted, the tests confirmed that I was having a serious heart attack. I was admitted and they stabilized me. Dye was injected and they conducted a cardiac catheterization procedure. A small hole was cut into my femoral artery in my groin and they ran a small camera up to my heart to see any blockages. As I lay there watching the monitor, I could see the blockages. Dr. Douglas Anderson of Paradise, California saw three, maybe four blockages. Being a double transplant recipient, the doctors wanted me to go to the medical center in San Francisco for my heart surgery. Dr. Hill, a heart transplant specialist, was assigned to me. He came to see me just before surgery. I reminded him that we are not doing a heart transplant, just a repair job! In August of 1998 I had a quadruple heart by-pass. The doctors took veins out of my legs and by-passed the heart vein blockages. My heart was stopped for five and a half hours, the work completed and then my heart restarted.

My right hip replacement that was done in 1979 had loosened. I was in extreme pain and needed my right hip revised. In November of 1998, just 3 months after a quadruple heart by-pass, I was in surgery to revise my right hip. Before I went into surgery at California Pacific Medical Center, Pacific Campus in San Francisco, I asked my surgeon, Dr. Lin Ho, if I could have my stainless steel prosthesis he was taking out. He said I could if he could autoclave it to sterilize it. When I woke up in Recovery Room, Dr. Ho was standing at my left side with my old hip in a sealed plastic bag. My recovery and rehabilitation went well. Over time I healed and was walking again without crutches.

One day in March of 1999, I began to itch severely. Antihistamines did not work to calm the itching. I was scheduled to have right knee surgery to repair the Anterior Crucia Ligament (ACL) that I tore many years before. As I lay in the Pre-Op room at UCSF Moffit Medical Center awaiting knee surgery, a nurse noticed my itching and also that I was turning yellow! They did tests and quickly found I had a blocked bile duct. I could not have the knee surgery, they needed to immediately open the bile duct or I would die!

To open my bile duct was not going to be easy, they tried going down my esophagus through my stomach and to the blockage. My bile duct would not open this way. Next, they made an incision in my right rib cage and went in and through my liver to the blockage. My bile duct would not open this way. Their only option was to totally open my abdomen up, they cut through my stomach muscle to access the blockage site. This was a big surgery as they totally removed the bile duct and connected my small intestine directly to the bottom of my liver where my bile duct was. It took a long time to recover from this due to the large incision through the stomach muscle.

Now that my body was functioning correctly again, we scheduled my knee surgery two months later for May. This time I was able to have my knee surgery. Everything went well with the exception that they were unable to reconstruct my ligament. I woke up with an Anterior Cruica Ligament transplant. Now, I had a kidney transplant, a liver transplant, and a knee ligament transplant. The recovery and rehabilitation went well, and I soon was off the crutches and walking again. I had a major surgery in August, November, March and then May! I must say, I was getting very tired of all the surgeries.

A year later, my left hip had loosened and I was ready to have my left hip revised. Hip replacements last about 8 to 10 years before they loosen and cause pain. My hip replacements lasted about 20 years, so I was very blessed for the longevity. I again asked Dr. Lin Ho of California Pacific Medical Center, Pacific Campus San Francisco if I could have my stainless steel prosthesis. He again told me I could if he could sterilize it in the autoclave. Unfortunately, he could not get the bottom half of my hip out. The bottom half is the stainless steel part that I wanted. The bottom half was in tight and only the top half, which is plastic and attached with screws had loosened. He revised it, and in the process of replacing it had to use cadaver bone grafts to reinforce my pelvis. Now I had a kidney transplant, a liver transplant, a knee ligament transplant and a bone graft, which is considered a tissue transplant and a bovine fistula from a bull in my left forearm. A part here, a part there, jokingly, it seemed like I was becoming Frankenstein! I light-heartedly take it all in stride and laugh at myself and how crazy it all has become.

Interviewer: Who drove you to and from these many surgeries you had?

Answer: *"A variety of people drove me. Mostly my mom and a good friend John Jans drove me to and from all my surgeries. They both know that when I get out of the hospital, the first stop I want to make is to get a hot fudge sundae. This is what I do to help myself relax and accept that I made it out of the hospital safe and sound."*

Interviewer: Have you ever been in a tunnel with a bright light drawing you to the other end?

Answer: *"No, I have not. Sometimes, I wish I would have been in such a tunnel. To have such a divine experience would be absolutely fabulous and life altering! I feel that I have gone where few men have gone in the medical world, but I have not been blessed with such an incredible experience."*

Interviewer: Have all these surgeries ever gotten you down where you wanted to commit suicide?

Answer: *"No, not at all. Suicide is not an option for me. I have always felt very protective of my kidney transplant, and I always did whatever I could to protect the kidney transplant. I feel that some loving person said "YES" to organ donation and they expect the recipient to take as good care as possible of the organ they received. I feel very responsible for the well being of the kidney and liver transplants I have received. To commit suicide would be not only killing myself, but would be killing my two organ transplants and I could never do that!"*

Interviewer: Do you know anything about your organ donors?

Answer: *"Yes I do. This answer may take awhile. I do not know anything about my kidney transplant of 1976. The California Transplant Donor Network is the organ procurement organization that matches up the deceased with the waiting patient. This organization did not start keeping records of who the organs went to until 1987. Because of this fact, I do not know anything about my kidney transplant of 1976. I only know that I had a great desire to build a sailboat and sail off into the sunset.*

I do know about my liver transplant in October of 1997. I was told that my liver was to come from a teenage boy who was shot in the back of the head. After six months, through a series of miraculous happenings, I found out I did not receive my liver from a teenage boy who was shot. For six months I was uneasy and kept feeling like something was wrong. I could not put my finger on what the problem was.

In April of 1998, I had a very unusual dream. I was dreaming there was a beautiful teenage Hispanic girl with an ear to ear grin sitting in a chair in my room reading my book about neuro-peptides (memory cells). I had been waiting to get my hips revised and a knee surgery, so when I got out of bed it was very, very slowly and with an extreme amount of pain. I woke up standing up, yelling, "Mary, no, Maria! Mary, no, Maria!" It was a very surreal dream. The next day, I was doing a story for our trans-plant support group's newsletter. I was inter-viewing a heart recipient at her house and saw an invitation to a memorial service for Northern California organ donor families. There were two numbers on the invitation to make your reservations, one in Modesto, California, and one in San Francisco. I had previously been in contact with the San Francisco office a few times, but this time for an unexplainable reason I called the Modesto office. Trace'e Harris answered my call. I told her I received a liver transplant in October and would like to make reservations to attend Northern California's annual organ donor family memorial service. Trace'e immediately started to ask me questions to which she already knew the answers. She asked me questions of my age, my children and where I lived. I asked her how she knew these facts about me. She replied that she believes she has my file in her hands at this moment! She needed to know more strictly personal information about me so she could verify this folder she was holding was mine. After some research and verification, she was right. The donor family was going to the memorial service and wanted to meet me.

Trace'e Harris asked me more questions but this time about my donor. I told her I was told my donor was a teenage boy shot in the head, but I was unsure and didn't think my liver came from him. I told her I felt my liver came from a teenage girl from the central valley near Fresno, California. She said I was "Correct so far, except she had lived in Modesto about 100 miles north of Fresno". Trace'e then asked me what she looked

81

like, and I described the beautiful Hispanic girl in my dreams just a few days ago. Trace'e had a photo of my donor and confirmed that I was describing my donor exactly! She then told me her name, Anita Maria Holguin, and that she never wanted to be called just Anita, but Anita Maria! I had my dream a few days before and awoke saying Mary, no, Maria! I think my chin was down on my chest with astonishment.

I brought my long time friend Luisa Garza to the California Transplant Donor Network's memorial service with me as I was very nervous. When we met my donor family, another fantastic thing happened. Luisa and my donor mom knew each other from years ago! What a small world we live in."

Chapter 8

Cancer

⌁

"Cancer, the dreaded "C" word of death! Organ transplant recipients are prone to cancer as a result of the anti-rejection drugs we have to take. I developed a crusty spot on the bottom of my right eyelid. My doctor told me it was cancerous and he would have to surgically remove my bottom eyelid and replace it with skin from behind my ears. My new eyelid did not have eyelashes and did not look very good.

I now had dry spots on my scalp. The doctor told me the dry spots were cancerous. My doctor surgically removed three of the spots that were cancerous. I had never dealt with cancer. This was something totally new to me. After the three surgery sites were healed, the cancer came back!

Now a more aggressive treatment was needed. A series of radiation treatments were scheduled. I went through the radiation treatments, they made my head burn from the inside out. The radiation was so aggressive it made my skin slough off as if it were melted. A few weeks after completing the treatments, a large bump suddenly came up. The cancer was back! Surgery was the only option to rid me of this killer cancer.

All of my skin was removed from my scalp down to my skull. My skull was now totally exposed. They could not put a skin graft on it, they had to let it heal by itself. Being immuno-suppressed (due to my organ transplants) and the extreme radiation treatments, made it almost impossible to grow new skin. The hole has slowly filled in but is still the size of a quarter. At the time of the writing of this book, it has been almost seven years and I still have exposed skull!

Both of my right eye lids started to have dry crusty spots on them. You guessed it, more cancer. The decision to do radiation instead of surgery was made. The radiation was a long and arduous journey. The radiation made my entire head, especially the left side where I was previously radiated, feel on fire. My right eye, my sinuses and the left side of my head had to be packed in blue ice. It felt like I had poured hot sauce in my right eye and packed peppers up my nostrils!

I had eight months of long-suffering; the pain and heat would not go away. My right eye had to be surgically removed to stop that heat and tremendous pain. I never imagined I would go through life with just one eye. Now, I'm known as the guy with the eye patch. Kind of cute though, I look like a mysterious pirate.

Being a kidney transplant patient, I have monthly lab work done which includes a urinalysis. A few months after I lost my eye, my lab work showed blood in my urine. That blood was tested and showed to be cancerous. It was transitional bladder cancer!

My kidney transplant was starting to have problems. My urine could not drain out from my kidney into my bladder. Cancer had blocked the ureter tube between my kidney and my bladder. I had to have a tube placed through my abdomen that went directly into the kidney to drain my urine. I now had a urine bag. It is crucially important to keep the tube that goes through my abdomen absolutely clean of bacteria.

After returning home one afternoon, I suddenly was very sick, shaking, with a fever and vomiting. I went to bed very sick and woke up the next morning even sicker. My mom drove me to the emergency room of John C. Fremont Hospital in Mariposa, California. By the grace of God, the emergency room physician was trained at a major medical center in San Francisco. He instantly diagnosed me properly. I had the deadly sepsis.

Sepsis is a bacterial infection of the blood. It is extremely serious and quickly infected my organs. It can kill a person in eight to ten hours! I felt very bad, but I did not think I was as close to death as the doctor knew I was. The doctor told me and my parents many times that he did not know if they could save me.

The emergency Medi-Flight helicopter was called in to fly me to California Pacific Medical Center, Pacific Campus in San Francisco. In the helicopter at 2500 feet the flight nurse also told me they didn't know if they could save me. Once we landed at the airport and I was in the ambulance, the paramedic told me he did not know if they could save me. By now, I was getting very tired of hearing that they may not be able to save me.

I was placed in Med-Surg ICU, where the most critical patients are. The doctors and nurses told me they were not sure they could save me. I now realized how critical I was. I arrived in the early evening and they worked on me until 2:30 in the morning. I fell asleep and awoke early in the morning.

I instantly sensed something was wrong! There was an evil presence swirling around my feet that made me very anxious! I hardly know how to describe the two black, small tubular ghostlike figures with large eyes and large mouths laughing at me. I had an inherit sense that they were demon spirits laughing at me because they were going to finally kill me. Satan was tormenting me with his chilling evil. I was scared!

Suddenly, there was a presence behind me at my right shoulder. I could not see to my right as I am blind in my right eye, but I felt there was a huge warrior guardian angel sent to protect me. This guardian angel did not have long blond hair, a chiffon dress and feathered wings. This guardian angel was over seven tall and a big strong warrior in full armor ready to do battle! Now, I felt another huge guardian angel on my left side, he too was ready to do battle! I felt like John Wayne had just arrived with the cavalry, in the nick of time. Suddenly, those ghostly figures swirling around my feet disappeared!

I felt fine, I sat up in bed, my fever was gone, and my tremors were gone. God saved me from demonic forces and healed me once again. I asked the doctor, "If someone survives, how long will they be in the hospital?" He responded, "About two to three weeks." I was out of the hospital in 2 1/2 days! This was a life-altering experience for me. It helped me to accept the power of God. I know now that there is nothing too wonderful to be true. All things, including miracles, are possible through God! I am living proof that God still performs miracles!

After trying to kill the bladder cancer with chemotherapy that did not work, I required surgery. In the summer of 2005, I had a major surgery that took out my two native kidneys that were left in me in 1976 when I received my kidney transplant. Then, I had another major surgery that removed my prostate gland, bladder and kidney transplant at the UCSF, Moffitt Medical Center.

My dear friend Mike Decker traveled 200 miles to San Francisco, got a hotel room, and visited me for three days straight. He kept telling me that "God was going to totally heal me." The doctors did all they could to remove all my cancer. They were optimistic that they had removed it all. I had a CT scan a few months later to make sure all of the cancer was gone. The CT scan came back bad. I had cancerous tumors all around the outside of my intestines, up the insides of both of my rib cages, and three tumors on the bottom of my liver transplant. I was inoperable! To say the least, I was not a happy camper. Once again, I was looking at death. The only medical treatment available was chemotherapy.

I now was on hemodialysis (kidney machine) as they had removed my kidney transplant and I had no kidney function. The doctors did not know how much chemotherapy to give me as the hemodialysis would take most of the chemotherapy out of me and it would not affect the cancer properly. They gave me very large doses and crossed their fingers that it would work.

Over the spring and early summer of 2006 the chemotherapy made me sicker and sicker. The tumors around my intestines were squeezing my intestines and causing partial bowel obstruction. I could only eat a little applesauce and Jell-O. The doctors put me on a high protein, high nutrition drink so I would not get malnourished. I never wanted to eat, I had to force myself to eat. I was extremely ill, the intense pain in my abdomen was becoming too much to handle.

I live in a cottage behind my landlord's, Dominic and Pat Nastri. Pat took me under her wing and made sure anything I needed was done! Morphine was not doing the trick. The ambulance took me to the hospital a variety of times when I thought I would die. I kept thinking how Mike Decker told me God would totally heal me. I was too sick and too fatigued to pray anymore. It seemed that Mike was wrong.

The last time the ambulance took me to the hospital, I was sure I would die during the night. I had a high fever, the tremors, tachycardia (a fluttering heart beat that does not pump blood properly and organ failure can occur), respiratory distress, and agonizing pain throughout my abdomen. I was so wrong! God once again healed me. I woke up in the morning totally healed! My fever was gone, my tremors were gone, my tachycardia was gone, I was breathing normally, and my excruciating abdominal pain was gone!

I woke up as the hospitality lady brought in my breakfast tray. I was frustrated that she brought in a normal diet tray. I needed my applesauce, Jell-O and high protein drink. For the first time in three months food smelled good to me. My stomach growled and said it was hungry. This was a strange sensation to me. I told myself not to listen to my stomach. I knew if I ate this food it would come back up. The food smelled good, my stomach growled again. Noticing my fever was gone, my tremors were gone, and the agonizing pain was gone, I decided to take a small bite. I waited awhile and took a second bite, then a third bite. I was back to normal. I realized God blessed me again with a healing as I was sleeping! Mike was right. God did totally heal me! God is so good.

Interviewer: Have you ever been told that you are one of God's angels?

Answer: *"Yes, a lady did tell me once that I was one of God's angels. I really don't believe I am one of God's angels. I do believe I held the hand of one of His angels. I also think that I am here to be a servant and help people with their lives. I just love helping people in any way that I can. When I help people, I am the happiest I can be.*

I believe God wants me to be a servant to mankind in the organ transplant world now that I have so much expertise in that area. He has put the idea of HealthQuest House Foundation in my heart. I now have the complete confidence and passion to complete the mission God wants me to do with my life."

Interviewer: Why is it so important for you to give so much back to the organ transplant community?

Answer: *"Since I was 18 years old, I have been in the organ transplant world. I feel such a deep love for my organ donor families and everyone who helped me. I want to do all I can to show my love back to them. Receiving an organ transplant saved my life twice. Many of my friends have died waiting for a life-saving organ transplant. I will always do what I can to increase organ donor awareness and organ donations.*

I have been an advocate for organ donation since I was 18 years old. I am now 51 years old. I have conducted speaking presentations at

*numerous high schools, colleges, clubs and orga-
nizations over many years. I was giving organ
donor awareness presentations to the public
long before anyone knew that they could donate
their organs and save somebody's life. Once the
California Transplant Donor Network estab-
lished itself with a solid volunteer organ donor
awareness program, organ transplants were then
more realized and accepted as the word got out
that organ transplants really do work and work
well.*

Interviewer: What does HealthQuest House
Foundation really mean to you personally?

Answer: *"HealthQuest House Foundation means
everything to me because the idea came from
God through me. I saw a gap in the healthcare
system concerning organ transplant patients,
and I decided to fill that gap. We will assist
organ transplant patients and their required
support personnel with overnight accommodations, transportation, proper nutrition, a safe
environment, organ transplant education, insurance education, and meet their spiritual needs
at a HealthQuest House Facility that will be
within 50 miles of an accredited organ transplant medical center. Our first facility is planned
to be in the South San Francisco, California,
area. After that, the next facility I plan to open*

will be near the University of Washington. There will only be a $10 per night charge per room. We are a non-profit foundation and all positions are volunteer, so we will be continually doing fundraising activities, applying for grants and securing sponsorships to raise money to expand with new facilities. We will be changing lives and saving lives, while saving souls."

Interviewer: What is your vision for the future of HealthQuest House Foundation?

Answer: *"The Vision Statement of HealthQuest House Foundation is...The vision of HealthQuest House Foundation is to be a steward of service to humanity in the organ transplant arena with overnight accommodations and services. The HealthQuest House vision also includes expanding our facilities and services throughout the world and to advocate organ donor awareness. Promoting American patriotism and providing Christian stewardship with compassion and integrity above reproach, for all that we do is for the glory of God."*

Interviewer: With the loss of one eye, do you see more beauty in life than people with two eyes?

Answer: *"Yes, I think I see more beauty in life than most people. It is not only due to the fact that I have only one eye; it is because of all the medical adversities I have gone through. I look for what is beautiful in people. Many look for what they can criticize about someone. Part of the beauty of life is not only taking the time to enjoy the small aromatic flowers, but choosing the way you live. You can live by chance or you can live by choice. I choose the way I live so there is very little chance in my life.*

There is a special place in my heart that this world's reality cannot touch. At this special place you will find my faith. I am a many-faceted person and most people only see one of my many brilliant sides that God has given me. I feel that my body is a temple; my scars are just the wallpaper on the walls."

Interviewer: What can a newly transplanted organ transplant patient do to have a more successful transplant?

Answer: *"There are a variety of things they can do to make their transplant more successful. They can be sure to do all their lab work when they are required to do it, make all of their doctor appointments and take all their medications as prescribed. Also, live a healthy life style, being very aware of bacterial and viral infections, as their immune system is suppressed and they can easily catch a life-threatening bacterial or viral infection. They should exercise regularly, get ample sleep and rest time, avoid stress, eat healthy living foods, take high quality vitamin and mineral supplements, drink purified water and breathe purified air.*

The air and water around us is really, really bad and getting worse. There are high quality water and air purification systems that work marvelously! As a patient, you and your support person need to be pro-active and learn all you can about your medical challenge and your environment around you."

Interviewer: Do you have friends who don't believe in God?

Answer: *"Sure I do. Some of my very best friends that I love the most, don't believe that God exists. We live in America and we have freedom of religion to believe in God or chose not to believe in God."*

Chapter 9

My Friends Speak Out

≈

I have chosen four friends to each write a 500 - 1000 word essay about what they think about me and how I respond to adverse challenges. My four wonderful friends are Luisa Garza, Linda Twehous, Michael Decker and Tracy Tice. I did notice that the ladies wrote a good amount about me and the gentlemen wrote only a short bit. These essays have not been altered or corrected in any way, they are exactly as written by my wonderful friends

Luisa Garza

"My friend Steve is one of the most positive human beings I have ever had the pleasure to know. We were friends in High School back in the mid 70's. He was usually a smart-alec and to a degree he still is. He has a witty sense of humor and he cracks me up. I often have conversations with him and listen in disbelief about what new medical journey he has been experiencing. There is one conversation in particular in which I will never forget. The exact year escapes me but I got a call at home and it went something like this:

"Hey Lui, Guess what?"

"I don't know Steve? You won the lottery?"

"Guess where I am?"

"Hawaii?"

"No, I just had a heart attack and I am in Feather River Hospital waiting to be transported to SF!"

He takes my breath away. He had a *major* heart attack and needed a quadruple bi-pass! The heart attack and a majority of his medical problems are associated with side affects of the meds he takes so his body will not reject his organ transplant. It has either been his knees, hips or liver deteriorating, the heart attack and skin cancer (since he was 19 after he received the kidney transplant) that has caused one medical emergency after the other.

I listened in disbelief; he sounded so matter-of-fact; as though he really was in Hawaii telling me a tall tale. This is how Steve is – always positive! He was never a 'woe is me' kind of guy. I think he has learned to take all of this life and death exciting events as just a part of life. Don't get me wrong, he wants to live and this might explain why he is here to this day – our million dollar man! I have never met one single person who has experienced the constant life threatening or family trauma as Steve has. I have met people who have gone through a lot less and they are depressing people. There is something completely different about Steve. He has in immense reservoir of love and patience that he draws upon allowing him to successfully move from one ordeal to the next.

He really just wants to work on his dreams and see his visions come to fruition. The medical stuff constantly creates setbacks but as soon as he can; he gets right back on the horse and moves forward on his projects. I believe everything he says. One day he told me he was going to start a foundation to help others in need of organ transplants, then I got a call that he was back in the hospital with skin cancer complications that ultimately resulted in the loss of one eyeball. Within weeks of that event passing and he regained his strength, he called to say that he is one step closer to creating the Health Quest Foundation and has his Board of Directors and Mission Statement in place. Plus, he told me he was getting custom eye patches made and made pirate 'arh, arh, arh" noises!

In spite of Steve's medical history, he will try his best to help others out. No matter if he has never met or heard of you. The gift he is to the world is the love he freely gives. He will attend the Organ Transplant meetings and talk to people about their upcoming transplants even if he is feeling terrible. I suppose his experiences, and his willingness to share has probably helped hundreds of people find the strength and resources they need to get through their own transplant.

He invited me to drive him and attend a Transplant Reunion in which he would get to meet the family that made it possible for him to live when he needed a liver transplant. As we were driving down he told me about some dreams he had in which he woke up in the middle of the night after a dream and shouted out "Maria!" he envisioned a young person sitting on a chair in front of him in his room. He always thought he had received the liver from a young boy who had been shot. Turns out it was a young Mexican girl and her middle name was Maria! It gave us the opportunity to discuss how transplant recipients can sometimes feel something related to the person whose organ is now transplanted. He began craving Mexican and spicy food prior to learning about Maria and since that is not his favorite food it was quite a surprise. The reunion was very emotional and heartfelt for me. It convinced me there is so much love and generosity in the world. I know there are shortages of organs available, but when a family makes that difficult choice you can feel the love. We watched a video that the donor families submitted of their loved ones life and you could feel their presence in the room. Meeting the family of 'Maria' was quite an experience as well. I realized that even when a family makes the decision to donate it can be exceedingly difficult for them still. I am thankful for their courage.

When Steve received that transplant it was probably the first time he really wanted to die. He was in agonizing pain, and had been deprived of oxygen by a nursing mistake and felt as if all of his efforts to stay alive were too much. He told me a little angel sat on his bed, she cried and told him she loved him and for him to please stay alive. Naturally, knowing Steve, he tapped deep into that reservoir of his and made a come back. Turns out that little angel was the daughter of another transplant recipient! There are angels among us and I believe this child talking to Steve was only one angel talking to another angel. He re-evaluated his life after that dramatic episode and from it came a deeper meaning of his purpose. That purpose has been to serve the transplant community and the creation of the Health Quest Foundation. Having Steve in my life is a treasured gift. Even though we don't see each other frequently, when we do get together it is as though no time has passed. My life is enriched because of his deep reservoir of love and commitment to live and his positive and silly attitude. I love you Steve"! *by Luisa Garza*

Linda Twehous:

"My name is Linda. When Steve asked me to contribute to his book, my first reaction was a feeling of honor, which quickly morphed into fear that I wouldn't do this wonderful friend justice with my words. As I sat and began organizing my thoughts,

I tried to mentally define Steve. He is honest, funny, courageous, stalwart in the face of adversity, faithful and loyal, not only to God, but also to his friends and to his family.

I have known Steve since the summer of 1967 when we met at Vacation Bible School, at the Little Church in the Hills, Mt. Bullion, California. My mother played the piano; his mother sang in the choir. We spent a lot of time together waiting for our moms. We also spent many years participating in the same church youth group. Steve has over the years filled the position of older, and in his opinion I'm sure, wiser brother. We have been friends for a very long time.

Steve has always faced physical challenges. Children can be cruel and since Steve is short of stature, with some dwarf characteristics, he was at times the brunt of other's character deficiencies. He met those challenges with a sunny outlook and won many of his detractors over to his point of view.

In high school Steve was a contributing member of the varsity wrestling team and surprised his opponents with his "moves." We used to run around in his '57 Chevy. It was black and shiny and could almost fly. I was shallow enough at that point to have been friends with him for his car if I hadn't been a genuine friend already! Our high school was small and everyone knew everyone else and of course knew their business too. Steve and I suffered through Spanish I, and Spanish II together, with La

Bruja as our instructor. Our friendship strengthened and he became *Esteban* to my *Leenda*.

In 1977 my husband Larry and I married and moved to San Francisco near Stanford Medical Center. During the time we lived there, Steve had one of his hip replacements. I can't remember now if it was pre-op or post-op when he stayed with us, but whichever it was, he was his normal entertaining self. I forgot to turn on the water heater in the water bed and he practically froze to death. Did he complain? No, however, I will likely never be allowed to forget the incident. My time-line is fuzzy these many years later, but I do believe it was the hip replacement wherein he contracted Hepatitis B through a contaminated blood transfusion. During our friendship, Steve has endured many difficulties. He received a kidney transplant. His other hip was replaced. His brother Mike died and his mother was killed in a traffic accident. Through it all, Steve has remained true to our Lord and positive in his dealings with others. I was present at his marriage and informed at the birth of each of his two children. We were in touch when his marriage dissolved during his battle with liver failure, caused by the Hepatitis B contracted during the hip surgery. My heart went out to him and when asked what Larry and I could do to help, Steve simply asked us to pray for him.

I recall speaking with Steve shortly after his liver transplant. He related to me an incident which occurred the day before his liver became available.

Steve was not in his room when his doctor made rounds and the room appeared to have been made ready for a new occupant. When the doctor went looking for answers to Steve's whereabouts, he met Steve in the hall with his IV pole, returning from the showers. The doctor informed Steve that his blood stats were so poor he should not be alive, not to mention walking in the hallway. Steve's reply, "Doc, God just isn't finished with me yet." Steve is so accepting of God's plan for his life. The caption on the picture Steve sent me of him with his diseased liver reads, "Yummmm, what's for dinner?" I know Steve has endured great physical as well as emotional pain, and many surgeries. I continue to be amazed and in awe of his perseverance and his soul-deep belief that each setback is only a new challenge which God will help him to overcome.

My son Joseph and I were in California on vacation when Steve had his heart by-pass surgery. My son's most vivid recollection of Steve's sense of humor is Steve cracking jokes as his monitors were going crazy with heart attacks while we were visiting him post-operatively! Joseph and Steve were trying to top each other with knock-knock and elephant jokes. I was freaking out and Steve was calm, telling us the medical staff was having trouble getting his medications regulated to stop the attacks, no big deal.

When my husband became an organ donor on July 1, 2001, it was a tribute to our friend Steve's activity on behalf of organ donation. Over the period of our adult friendship, the one regret Steve has expressed to me is that with all of the family members he has lost, not one organ has been donated. As part of Steve's "friend family," we have done our best to rectify this situation. My son and I are also designated organ donors upon our passing from this life.

Recently, Steve lost his right eye as the result of unsuccessful skin cancer radiation therapy. There was a bit of discouragement in his voice as he was relating the sequence of events to me. I was horrified and indignant on his behalf. In typical fashion, Steve spent part of the phone call soothing my ire and putting the most positive light possible on the situation. As we wrapped up our conversation, he chuckled and told me to look on the bright side. Pirates are looked upon with romance and admiration today and hey, with his eye-patch, he qualifies!

As I write my contribution to Steve's message to all of you, Steve is again facing enormous challenges. He is completing his second round of chemotherapy to fight a malignant tumor in his bladder. Is he defeated? Is he contemplating giving up? No, he is emailing me, his friend who is facing minor problems by comparison, and reminding me that those who walk in God's grace face challenges, not problems, trials, or tribulations. Honest, funny, courageous, stalwart in the face of adversity, faithful and loyal, this is my friend Steve". *By Linda Twehous*

Michael Decker

"We are all faced with challenges in this life, challenges that can make or break us.

Steve Cooke has chosen, with the grace of God, to face his many challenges and use them to encourage others and to grow into the man he is today.

Steve is a continuing blessing to me and others as an example of courage with good humor.

It is amazing to visit him in the hospital as he faces another negative prediction by doctors with faith and a confidence that **"And we know that all things work together for good to those who love God, to those who are called according to His purpose." Romans 8:28.** *by Michael Decker*

Tracy Tice

"I met Steve "Cookie" in the summer of '97 when he was in need of a liver transplant. The first thing I noticed about Steve was that he had a heart of gold. As I got to know Steve he seemed to have the ability to laugh at any circumstance. At that time I think he had gone through about 100 surgeries, always giving the glory to Jesus. One day as we were talking on the phone, Steve suffered a heart attack and he calmly said to me "Tracy I think I'm having a heart attack." I told him to call 911, he did and later that day I found out it was true when he called from the hospital. Steve reminds me of a Timex watch, he keeps on ticking (for Jesus!). Steve has the ability to see the 'big picture' whether he's doing physically good *or* bad. Because he knows the 'big picture' is eternal life with Jesus. As I write this today, April 3, 2007, Steve is battling a death sentence, cancer. Steve has a sense of humor and knows that God has one too, and as so many times before, he might even beat this cancer too! Lately in our phone conversations Steve is always up yet I never know if this will be the last time we'll talk here on earth but our conversations always end on that 'Good News' note of what Jesus has done for us. Steve has been one of those 'true' friends, which seems rare to find now a days. He has probably been through more medical procedures than anyone I know or will probably ever know. One thing I do know though, whether I do see Steve here again or not, I *will* see Steve again in heaven. Steve has been an inspiration to me and our friendship will *always be*". *By Tracy Tice*, Grove, Oklahoma, April 3, 2007.

Chapter 10

Question and Answer Session

Interviewer: Are you going to write an autobiography?

Answer: *"Yes, I would like to write my autobiography in 2008. One problem with my autobiography is it would take three books and, if Hollywood gets it, they would have to make a mini-series as it is so unique and complex.*

Now that this book is completed, HealthQuest House Foundation is currently at the top of my priority list. Helping organ transplant patients to more successfully survive an organ transplant has been in my heart for over 30 years. Once we open our first HealthQuest House facility, I would like to obtain a research grant to track the mortality rate of organ transplant patients in the medical transplant centers we serve, to see if our efforts are effectively lowering the mortality rate."

Interviewer: Do you ever feel like you have been in a medical war against your body?

Answer: *"Yes, I do feel that I have been in a medical war. Considering all the action I've seen, the left chest of my uniform would be overflowing with colorful ribbons of the battle campaigns I have fought. It would also be layered with medals of satin and glistening brass. The purple heart medals for being wounded in these medical wars would hang thick on my chest."*

Interviewer: What do you envision the afterlife to be?

Answer: *"I envision the afterlife for Christians to be so incredibly wonderful and beautiful that I would not be able to describe the beauty of it all! The Bible describes a little of it in Revelation 21-22."*

Interviewer: When the little angel held your hand at the side of your bed, what was going through your head?

Answer: *"When I realized that the nurse standing at my side was not a nurse but a Heavenly Angel sent to comfort me, I was awestruck and dumbfounded. I kept asking myself, "Did what occurred, really happen?" This was the first time anything divine like this had ever happened to me. Also, when April Lynn was at my bedside after my liver transplant I had a warm fuzzy feeling of complete overwhelming comfort with her. When I tell my doctors about my Angels and Jesus coming to me, most of them dismiss what I experienced as hallucinations."*

Interviewer: Have there been many or any outstanding nurses or doctors who have inspired you or showed tremendous compassion and competence that really affected you?

Answer: *"Yes, certainly! With my kidney trans-plant, the surgeons, Dr. Oscar Salviateri and Dr. Nicholus Fuduska at the University of California, San Francisco, Moffitt Medical Center kept a very close and concerned eye on me. Also, the physicians, Dr. Flavio Vincinti and Dr. William C. E. Amend, as well as the attentive nurses were always there and available.*

During my liver transplant, the fantastic surgeons at California Pacific Medical Center, Pacific Campus, were Dr. John Roberts, Dr. Adil 'Ed' Walkile, Dr. Robert Osario and Dr. Chris Freise. The physician that I still see for my liver transplant is William Gish, M.D. He is awesome as is my nurse coordinator Karen Devaney, R.N., M.S.N."

Interviewer: How does one obtain miraculous heal-
ings like the ones you have experienced?

Answer: *"Wow, that's a complicated one! I don't
think a miracle must have a set of criteria to hold
to. God can give a miracle at anytime, anywhere,
to anyone. I start off in prayer in Jesus' name,
asking God for the healing I need. There is
power in Christian prayer. I ask as many friends
as I can to pray also for my healing. I think that
the important things in life take more time and
prayer, so we need to pray again and again for
our healing. Then, have the unyielding faith to
thank God again and again for the healing He is
giving us as we wait for it to finalize.*

*I also try to be the best Christian I can. When
you were a child, your father here on Earth probably didn't give you what you wanted if you were
bad. The same goes for your Father in Heaven. I
don't expect to be a carnal Christian and receive
blessings from God. Nothing is too wonderful
to come true. All things, including miracles, are
possible through God."*

Interviewer: Have you ever received bad information off the Internet?

Answer: *"Yes, I have seen bad information on the
Internet. The bad information and rumors seems
to be in the chat rooms and personal web sites. I*

have never seen any bad information or rumors on quality medical web sites. I will list some at the end of this book. With these web sites you can always depend on getting truthful, quality information."

Interviewer: Did you ever have anyone or anything to live for that helped you to survive?

Answer: *"Yes, the two most profound times were with my kidney and liver transplants. I was raised in the country with my grandparent's home just 150 feet away. My grandparents were an integral part of my upbringing and I kept telling myself, "I am going to survive so I can see them again." With my liver transplant, I had my children Stacey and David heavy on my heart, and all I wanted was to live to see them again."*

Interviewer: How many surgeries do you think you have had?

Answer: *"I was waiting for this question. I do not count dental surgeries or cryo-surgeries. As far as I know, I have had approximately 140 surgeries. Many, many of them have been small surgeries, but, as you have read, a fair amount of my surgeries have been pretty spectacular ones! I definitely feel that I am a champion of individu-*

ality. I am a many faceted man and know that most people only see one of my many sides."

Interviewer: What is you favorite scripture?

Answer: *"Isaiah 40:31 is my favorite scripture. While awaiting my liver transplant at California Pacific Medical Center, Pacific Campus, San Francisco, children in the hospital had made small wall plaques with sayings on them. They hung in the long hallways we walked at night for our exercise. Night after night, as I struggled to walk down the hall, I read "But those who wait on the Lord shall renew their strength; they shall mount up with wings like eagles, they shall run and not be weary, they shall walk and not faint." This scripture was very relevant as I needed my strength renewed, and I wanted to walk and not faint. Fainting was a big challenge for me. All I wanted was to be feeling well and see Stacey and David again."*

Interviewer: How bad is the food in the hospitals?

Answer: *"Most of the time the food is so-so. The taste of the food depends on how I feel and if I am on a restricted diet. At times, the food can be extremely good as this menu shows from California Pacific Medical Center, Pacific Campus, San Francisco."*

Interviewer: Over the years have you done much charitable work within your community?

Answer: *"Yes I have! One of the areas that stand out in my mind is the Mariposa County Sheriff's Department put bumper stickers on their vehi-*

cles that promoted organ donation. Sheriff James Allen and I are shown at the conclusion on the ceremony."

Chapter 11

My Reason for Being

*"HealthQuest House Foundation and this book are the two main reasons I believe God has kept me alive. My children are also the reason for me to still be alive. Servitude is something I really enjoy. Giving to others by being **other-centered** is a high for me. The following are the Mission Statement and the Vision Statement of HealthQuest House Foundation."*

Mission Statement

The mission of HealthQuest House Foundation will be to support the pre-organ transplant patients, post-organ-transplant recipients and their required support personnel with lodging, nutrition, transportation, safety, organ transplant education, medical center requirements and spiritual counsel as deemed necessary by the HealthQuest House management within a 50 mile radius of an accredited organ transplant medical center.

Vision Statement

The vision of HealthQuest House Foundation is to be a steward of service to humanity in the organ transplant arena with overnight accommodations and services. The HealthQuest House Foundation vision also includes expanding our facilities and services throughout the world and to advocate organ donor awareness. Promoting America patriotism and providing Christian stewardship with compassion and integrity above reproach, for all that we do, is for the glory of God.

Chapter 12

Healing Scriptures

"Here are just a few scriptures that speak about healing. I don't know why some people with infirmities are healed and others are not healed. I do know that I must pray in total faith and have my friends pray in faith for me. Healing is one of God's blessings. To obtain the full blessings of God, I also must try to maintain all of God's laws."

All Scripture is from the New King James Version of the Holy Bible

Is anyone among you sick? Let him call for the elders of the church, and let them pray over him, anointing him with oil in the name of the Lord. And the prayer of faith will save the sick, and the Lord will raise him up. And if he has committed sins, he will be forgiven. Confess your trespasses to

one another, and pray for one another, that you may be healed. The effective, fervent prayer of a righteous man avails much.
James 5: 14-16

Bless the Lord, O my soul, And forget not all His benefits: Who forgives all your iniquities, Who heals all your diseases, Who redeems your life from destruction, Who crowns you with lovingkindness and tender mercies, Who satisfies your mouth with good things, So that your youth is renewed like the eagle's.
Psalms 103: 2-5

But those who wait on the Lord Shall renew their strength; They shall mount up with wings like eagles, They shall run and not be weary, They shall walk and not faint.
Isaiah 40:31

Surely, He [Jesus Christ] has borne our griefs And carried our sorrows; Yet we esteemed Him stricken, Smitten by God, and afflicted. But He was wounded for our transgressions, He was bruised for our iniquities; The chastisement for our peace was upon Him, And by His stripes we are healed.
Isaiah 53: 4-5

He sent His word and healed them, And delivered them from their destruction.
Psalm 107: 20

Chapter 13

Quotes

"The *following are some quotes that I have written down over many, many years when I thought of them. Usually, I was inspired by someone or some event that had me slow down and take a closer look at who we really are."*

Live each and everyday as if you knew you only have one year left to live.

When you look life in the face, you can see the past. When you look death in the face, you can see your future.

One of the similarities we all have within us is the desire to be loved.

You need to maintain or regain your self-esteem. You are worth a good life. Give back to your community a part of what you have been so graciously given.

This book will only give you a small sniff of the overwhelming aroma of the wonderful miracles that have happened to me.

As a Christian, I see with the eye of faith and not fear.

People get so busy trying to attain what they think success is, they forget to enjoy their life.

You can live by chance or by choice.

Your life can be full of purpose or full of uncertainty, it's your choice.

Faith and patience go hand in hand.

If you never stop trying to achieve the next step forward you will always be successful.

There is an aura of energy around every person. Choose to be around positive energy people.

The most negative person in your life is probably you! If not, get some new friends!

Life threatening medical issues have allowed me to be in a position to appreciate life's smallest wonders.

My body is my temple, my scars are the wallpaper.

There is a place in my heart that this world's reality cannot touch. At this spot I find my deep neverending faith.

Setbacks are always part of the journey we are on. Expect to claim some defeats and go on to your destination.

Empty conquests, no matter how desirable, are just like another Chinese dinner. After you have been fulfilled, an empty feeling soon overcomes you.

Don't take inventory of what you have lost. Take inventory of what you have left, and use what you do have left to do the best you can with what you have.

True success is only attained when spiritual maturity is fully developed.

Always be in thoughtful balance. Balance the heavy hard times with the easy happy times.

My course in life is set by my tongue, and the final destination is achieved by my thoughts.

The difference between an average person and a hero is that a hero has learned to face their fears with faith.

The world says, I'll believe it when I see it. I say, I can envision it and I do believe I can achieve it.

Give someone you love flowers when they are alive to appreciate them.

When you have a disability, you must concentrate and develop your abilities to compensate for what you lack.

A straight line journey is boring, unadventurous, and non-educational. The learned experience of the journey from one point to another is what you should be seeking. It is not important to get to your destination as quickly as possible but to get there with something learned.

Mountains are hard to climb and often may take a very long time to get to the top. If you properly studied the terrain, chart a climbing route and have thoughtfully brought along all the necessary items you would need to complete your journey, then you should reach the top as anticipated. Your experience getting to the top of the mountain will be more rewarding than the exhilaration of attaining the summit and the beautiful view it beholds.

A positive attitude is a catalyst that causes a chain reaction of events that creates extraordinary results.

In the past, I have been afraid of death, angry and defiant of death and now as I have grown, I am very much at peace with death.

I feel the donor family has made a heart-wrenching, bittersweet decision that is lovingly other-centered.

Self-knowledge is the path to great heights of physical and spiritual awareness.

The words you speak are like a picture frame that shows the person you really are.

When I die, I will have succumbed to an offer I could not refuse.

When you see no boundaries, you can soar to heights beyond your wildest dreams.

Do more with your life than to just be breathing, be living!

Be a better person than you should be! Your dysfunctional past should have no bearing on who you are now.

Physical, emotional and spiritual health are each as important as the other. Missing or lacking in one of these health areas will keep you out of balance.

When you run out of time, buy some! If your career takes up all of your day, then hire someone to help you with some of the housework, filing papers or whatever it takes to regain your quality time with God and your family.

A local organ transplant support group is invaluable! Speaking with others who have gone through what you are about to go through is a true blessing.

The human will to live is an individual and inherent strength that cannot be measured by any device. I do not think about mine. I don't know why I have such a high level of the will to live.

God made us unique and perfect in His eyes. Our mannerisms and personality are for a purpose beyond our understanding. The one thing that is never changing is that I am always changing. I desire to develop myself into a better Christian with more truth and understanding of how God wants me to be, together with my born personality.

God is love and He is perfect. His love is for each and everyone of us. We just need to accept it. God desires for us to have good health and be prosperous. God also has ultimate wisdom and knows that mankind needs to have visual and hands-on aids so we may realize that miracles can and do happen.

To have a more full life, quit saying, "I'm going to do this or that." Make detailed plans, write them down and do what it takes to fulfill your dreams. Life is fragile and in an instant, your dreams may never come to be, if you fail to follow them.

My legacy is proportional to the destiny I make for myself.

God has put me in the very unique position of being a medical marvel.

I believe I was born at exactly the right time and place to do great things in the organ transplant world.

When times get tough, just remember that each and every hour is just 60 short increments of time that you know you can get through.

As I think of where I was and where I am now, I also think of who I was and who I am now. Growth is a slow process for me. I will always attempt to grow and develop into a better person.

I have humor as a way of coping with my medical adversities. For me, it is essential to see the lighter side of my challenges and laugh at how crazy my medical situation has become.

Are you going to view and live your life from the top of a trash heap or from the top of a beautiful mountain?

I trust that somehow God will work my adversities out for my good, for God is good.

We are an echo unto ourselves. What we say returns as an echo does, and that echo tells us what we think of ourselves.

The realm of your possibilities are solely limited to your vision. Your vision is born from the creative spirit given to you by God.

When, finally, you run out of you, your ears will hear, your eyes will see and your heart will open wide to a new way of thinking.

Chapter 14

Poems and Prayers

~~

"Here are a few poems I have written over the years. Usually, I would write a poem when I was in a particular mood. I may have been in a sad mood, happy mood, thankful mood, thinking of a friend or of my love for my organ donor."

Daily Prayer

My Father God, I confess that I am a sinner and ask for Your merciful forgiveness of all my sins. I pray that You open my eyes of understanding. Also, I pray to be in uncommon favor with everyone I contact and that You daily lead me down a righteous path. Father God, supernaturally open the doors I need to enter and close those doors that I should not enter. Father God, release my Angels to do warfare for me and please show me all of my blessings that you have already bestowed upon me.

Father God, give me uncommon wisdom to apply all of my blessings accordingly and please reveal my planned anointing to me. Father God, I pray that You would cloak me with unlimited peace, joy and love and also bless me with the ability to forgive those who have wronged me and allow others whom I have wronged to forgive me. In the name of Your Son, Jesus Christ, I pray with thanksgiving. Amen!

Thank You, God

My Father God, I thank You for the restful night You have given me, I thank You for the peace that You will give me today. I thank You for the prosperity that You have given me. I thank You for the wealth that You have given me. I thank You for my good health that You have given me. I thank You for the uncommon favor coming today. I thank You for giving me the understanding of others. I thank You for giving me wisdom. I thank You for all of my blessings. I thank You for Your mercy. I thank You for Your grace and I thank You for sacrificing Your son for me. I pray with thanks in the name of Your son, Jesus Christ. Amen!

Friendship

You are a friend indeed,
You are a friend I need,

I pray you are my friend for life,
No matter what my troubles or strife,

Whenever I need a hand to hold,
You've been there shining like gold.

Friendship is very special to me,
I've truly been blessed with a friend like
thee,
When two are introduced, a friendship
begins,
Forever we'll be friends, when God steps in,

You pray for me and I'll pray for you,
Life is so much nicer with a friend like you,

Loyalty to you friend, is deep within my
heart,
I trust God will see that we never part,

All I can say about a friend like you,
To me…you are a friend who is true blue!

Transplanted
(published 1999 Ceremony of Recognition by
California Transplant Donor Network)

My life was as normal as could be,
All was fine and I so very happy,

Yes, I was content if I can be so bold,
I'll never forget the day I was told,

An organ transplant was needed or I would
die!
Shocked with fatalism, I started to cry,

What about my work, my children, my wife?
Will this illness be the end of my life?

The world of medicine, now I was in,
Dear God, be with me, as I begin,

Lab tests, x-rays and medicine to take,
Doctors, nurses and appointments to make,

Being on a special diet as fatigue sets in,
I'm sick of being sick, will it ever end?

Day after day, I lay in my hospital bed,
Awaiting an organ transplant or I'll be dead!

Life soon over, this country boy from the
ridge,
My last breath overlooking the Golden Gate
Bridge,

While tragedy devastates a family with
strife,
Their decision to donate will save my life!

A legacy of their loved one now lives on,
The "Gift of Life" made my illness be gone,

Comfort I pray, for my donor family,
Their hurt I ask God to lift, as they grieve,

The love I have for my heroes is immense,
That horrible accident will never make
sense,

I promised my donor that I would help
humanity,
To make this world a better place to be,

In Heaven their Angel knows the love in their
heart,
The memories of their Angel will never part,

Someday in Heaven we shall all meet,
When that someday comes, it will be oh, so
sweet.

Chapter 15

Support Team, Support Groups and Patient Compliancy

Your strong support team is mandatory. Having a good attentive team of people who have your best interests at the heart of what they do is vitally important. It could mean the difference between life and death! The organ transplant medical center may have very few highly trained Registered Nurses and may work mostly with Nurses Aids to assist you. A Nurses Aid may be good-hearted but is extremely restricted with the duties they may offer you. This is an unfortunate financial decision that many medical centers are implementing.

Having people close to you with your best interests at heart should be an integral part of your overall plan of attaining your life-saving organ transplant. It doesn't matter what type of organ transplant you are seeking, you can never have enough people looking out for your well-being. You should have a well thought-out plan which includes financial support, support personnel, backup support personnel, transportation, insurance requirements, prescription education, medical education, nutritional education and most is a spiritual advisor. Have a *pre-transplant plan* in place and a *post-transplant plan* of success written out. Social workers are highly skilled and will assist you in constructing these plans.

Medical center organ transplant support groups are held at the organ transplant medical center and usually are specific to the type of organ transplant you are seeking. If you need a liver transplant then you would attend the Liver Transplant Support Group. These groups usually meet twice a week and attendance is required by most medical centers. These meetings are full of fantastic advice, so be sure your support person will take good notes. A social worker will probably oversee the group and keep it running efficiently.

Your local organ transplant support group is also of vital importance. Your local support group may be specific to a certain organ transplant or open to any type of organ transplant patient. Hopefully, you will have a support group within an easy drive so you can attend regularly. I started going to my support group when my medical center nurse coordinator suggested I do so. I thought I would not like attending this group, I was totally wrong!

I really enjoyed being able to speak with people who have been at the exact same medical center I was at and having the exact same organ transplant as I was to receive. It gave me great confidence to speak with people who have been there and successfully completed the organ transplant that I was about to do. Plenty of notes were taken at those invaluable meetings. Over the nine years at the Northern California Organ Transplant Support Group, I served as President, Secretary, Newsletter Editor and have been on the Speakers Bureau. I made many terrific friends and I hope you make wonderful friends at your support group.

Being a compliant patient is essential! You must keep all of your doctor's appointments, laboratory appointments, take all medicines as prescribed, and submit all paperwork required by your insurance company and the organ transplant medical center. Your cooperation in completing all appointments and tasks is mandatory! Why should the medical center give you a life-saving organ transplant if you are going to waste it by not taking your medications as prescribed? There are plenty of patients waiting to take your place for their life-saving organ transplant, and they will take their medications as prescribed.

Resources on the Web:

www.kidney.org
(National Kidney Foundation)

www.liverfoundation.org
(American Liver Foundation)

www.unos.org
(United Network of Organ Sharing)

www.healthquesthouse.com
(The Steven W. Cooke HealthQuest House
Foundation)

Epilogue

~

This book is not just about my medical history and where I have been, it is about my future and is the beginning of where I am going!

THIS BOOK IS DEDICATED IN LOVING MEMORY OF *ALL* ORGAN DONORS.

Contact Information

To contact Mr. Nastri for portraits, wildlife paintings or sketches contact Mr. Nastri at:

Mr. Dominic Nastri
5922 Sawmill Road
Paradise, California 95969

For more information about the Steven W. Cooke HealthQuest House Foundation or his book *'Conversations with a Masterpiece, Miracles and Medical Marvels'* contact Mr. Cooke *personally* at:

Steven W. Cooke
HealthQuest House Foundation
P.O. Box 726
Paradise, California 95967

www.healthquesthouse.com
healthquesthouse@sbcglobal.net

Printed in the United States
203139BV00001B/352-378/P

9 781604 775730